NETWORKING ARGUMENTS

PITTSBURGH SERIES
IN COMPOSITION,
LITERACY,
AND CULTURE

David Bartholomae and
Jean Ferguson Carr, Editors

NETWORKING ARGUMENTS

RHETORIC, TRANSNATIONAL FEMINISM, AND PUBLIC POLICY WRITING

REBECCA DINGO

UNIVERSITY OF PITTSBURGH PRESS

Published by the University of Pittsburgh Press, Pittsburgh, Pa., 15260

Manufactured in the United States of America
Printed on acid-free paper
10 9 8 7 6 5 4 3 2

Library of Congress Cataloging-in-Publication Data

Dingo, Rebecca Ann, 1975–
Networking arguments : rhetoric, transnational feminism, and public policy writing / Rebecca Dingo.
p. cm. — (Pittsburgh series in composition, literacy, and culture)
Includes bibliographical references and index.
ISBN 978-0-8229-6188-8 (pbk. : alk. paper)
1. Women—Social networks. 2. Sex role and globalization. 3. Rhetoric—Social aspects. 4. Rhetorical criticism. I. Title.
HQ1155.D56 2012
305.4—dc23 2012001781

TO ZAC WITH LOVE

CONTENTS

ACKNOWLEDGMENTS

Books are rarely written in isolation. Although words may be put on the page by a single person, for me, a wide community network of friends, colleagues, family members, and institutions enabled my writing of this book. I am indebted to this community, and I wholeheartedly thank you for your longtime support of my scholarly and personal development.

This project began, in a small way, through my contact with feminists and rhetoricians even in my early years in college at Miami University and in my studies at the Ohio State University. Emily Zakin, Carolyn Haynes, and Susan Jarratt planted the seed that I should be thinking about the relationships between language, power, and women's material circumstances. Nancy Campbell introduced me to critical feminist policy analysis, while Ara Wilson taught me how to account for transnational economic processes. Brenda Brueggemann, Wendy Hesford, and Nan Johnson guided me toward articulating a coherent relationship between rhetorical theory, feminism, and transnational studies. You are all truly the foundation to my scholarly work.

I am deeply appreciative of the University of Missouri and the Departments of English and Women's and Gender Studies who granted me several leaves and grants (especially, grants for travel and teaching releases from the Research Board and Research Council) to complete the research and writing of this project. My graduate students in my Rhetoric + Transnationalism course in 2008 and 2010 aided me in articulating clearly *why* we need a transnational feminist rhetorical analytic. In particular, Naomi Clark and I have had numerous conversations about transnational rhetorical analysis, and she also helped me with source sleuthing for this book. I am also sincerely grateful to the many warm and supportive colleagues with whom I have developed friendships over the years. Enid Schatz and Donna Strickland have not only been constant friends and part of my wide support system but they also were my cheerleaders and companions at Uprise Bakery (thanks too to Uprise and their staff!), where we would meet to write together. Knowing that you two were also toiling away alongside made writing feel easier and more purposeful. Thanks to you both for each reading and commenting on multiple drafts and chapters, and also thanks for providing occasional childcare when I needed a break or to catch up on work. Additionally, I am indebted to Donna's mindful writing practices: learning how to pause, take notice, breathe, and stop has changed my writing habits forever.

My scholarly community has widened significantly over the years of writing this book. I thank the Ohio State University's Women in Development Institute (WID), the University of Houston, and George Washington University for inviting me to present and workshop sections of this book. The comments I received at these talks certainly affected my arguments and ideas. Personally, I am genuinely and especially appreciative to Rachel Riedner, Bret Benjamin, Jen Wingard, Blake Scott, and Eileen Schell, who each provided, at different times throughout my writing process, ideas, comments, thoughts, and encouragement. Eileen and Blake, you two have served as occasional mentors for me, and I am deeply obliged for your willingness to answer professional and scholarly questions and for cheering on this project. Rachel and Bret, thank you for your thoughtful reviews and suggestions for the manuscript. And, Jen, I am so glad we have developed a friendship and scholarly support system for each other; I look forward to seeing your book in print too.

Last but certainly not least, I would not have been able to complete this manuscript without the everyday support and friendship of a variety of people. I wish to thank my mother (Barb Dingo) and mother-in-law (Dena Early) for your numerous trips out to the bellybutton of the nation to help with the house and childcare. Having the two of you come and play with Lucia, fold laundry, and make meals every so often certainly helped keep me (and my house) on track. Likewise, Tara Pauliny, Jen Phegley, and Lisa Tatonetti not only read drafts of this manuscript but they also made it possible for me to get away and have some down time. Kate Bedford provided me keen brilliance and biting English humor. Katarina Gephard read drafts and encouraged me along the way. Jason Palmeri and Leah Cheaney indulged my need to be creative outside of the academy; thank you for numerous conversations about food and drink, and thank you for the hours spent preparing meals and eating them. Leah, our friendship changed my life in CoMo; you made CoMo fun! Words cannot express how much I appreciated having your companionship. Zac Early and Lucia Dingo-Early have had to put up with late-night and weekend sessions away. I am grateful that the two of you have reminded me of the importance of balancing work and family and have made it easy to do so. Lucia, you have made it easy for me to stop and play. Zac, I dragged you to CoMo and through many ups and downs you have been constantly positive, loving, supportive, and patient, thank you.

NETWORKING ARGUMENTS

NETWORKING ARGUMENTS

> Global connections are everywhere.
> So how does one study the global?
>
> ANNA LOWENHAUPT TSING, *FRICTION*

NETWORKING ARGUMENTS: HOW RHETORICIANS SHOULD STUDY GLOBALIZATION

In 1995, delegates from 189 countries and territories and representatives from over 2,100 nongovernmental organizations (NGOs) travelled to Beijing for the Fourth World Conference on Women. Focusing specifically on mainstreaming women's needs into policy and development plans, this historic conference concentrated on the ways in which women's equality related to human rights as well as on women's ability to resist impoverishment, participate in public and private decision making, and influence media representations of women and girls. Participants took part in conversations and presented statements about women's struggles for gender equality and poverty alleviation. These statements provided a way for women's rights advocates to make connections among the struggles that women face across the globe.

One possible way to bring rhetorical theory to bear on globalization is to study rhetorical occasions such as the Beijing conference. Certainly, the Beijing conference was a momentous and unique event that brought women together from a variety of backgrounds, nations, and political agendas to conceive of a Platform for Action that would offer a plan to national and supranational policy makers for bringing women's issues and diverse needs to the center of policy making (*Beijing Declaration*).[1] Because delegates from each of the 189 nations and many representatives from several NGOs presented formal speeches that addressed the unique circumstances of women from that nation or organization, rhetoricians might consider, for example, who each country sent as a representative and what that representative spoke about. Or perhaps, rhetoricians might note the common themes or arguments that emerged across speeches or even how the speakers addressed international power relationships. Because the speeches at the Beijing conference were performative and celebratory, and they specifically called for gender mainstreaming alongside women's empowerment initiatives, this sort of occasion-bound rhetorical analysis might lead rhetoricians to conclude that the results of the Beijing conference were overwhelmingly positive. Certainly, as then First Lady Hillary Clinton aptly noted during her speech: "It is conferences like this that compel governments and peoples everywhere to listen, look, and face the world's most pressing problems." The Fourth World Conference on Women and the resulting Beijing Platform for Action did indeed influence how governments and global policy makers addressed women's poverty and disenfranchisement; post Beijing, several national governments and supranational organizations began to write gender mainstreaming imperatives into their own policies and development plans. Yet, as the rhetoric of gender mainstreaming traveled from policy to policy, development initiative to development initiative, policy and development experts reframed the meaning of gender mainstreaming to fit with their own agenda.

To really understand the rhetoric of gender mainstreaming, then, rhetoricians must look not only at static rhetorical occasions such as the Beijing conference but they must examine how rhetorics travel—how rhetorics might be picked up, how rhetorics might become networked with new and different arguments, and then how rhetorical meaning might shift and change as a result of these movements. In other words, analyzing the Beijing conference and the resulting Platform for Action as discrete texts only reveals a glimpse of the rhetoric of gender mainstreaming.

For example, while the Beijing Platform for Action offers a holistic and refined way of approaching gender inequalities, this sophisticated interpretation of what gender mainstreaming initiatives ought to do did not necessarily travel post Beijing as other organizations integrated the rhetoric of gender mainstreaming into their policy agendas. The definition of gender mainstreaming within the Beijing Platform reveals a nuanced definition that does not simply mean establishing policies that address gender disparities or examining how the policies will impact women and men differently. Rather, the Beijing Platform reflects transnational feminist goals and approaches by networking and linking the definition of gender mainstreaming to local and global structures that exacerbate inequalities, such as international trade agreements, (neo)colonial power relationships, changing local cultural practices, political unrest, and environmental degradation. The platform notes, for example, how globalization has affected women's well-being. It states, "since . . . 1985, . . . the world has experienced profound political, economic, social, and cultural changes, which have had both positive and negative effects on women" (*Beijing Declaration* 8). Among the negative effects that the platform mentions are "wars of aggression, armed occupation, civil wars, and terrorism" that often lead to "murder, torture, systematic rape, forced pregnancy and forced abortion," as well as "reduced . . . resources available for social development" (9). The Platform for Action also notes that gender discrimination is not due to the fact that women are ontologically *different* from men but that political practices and supranational development policies can *create* gender inequalities. Gender mainstreaming, according to the Beijing Platform, crucially means developing policies, programs, and practices that do not simply respond to gender inequality but that actually encourage social, cultural, and political practices that positively impact women and their diverse needs.

For this reason, the Beijing Platform explains how poorly designed structural adjustment policies, unequal education programs, excessive military expenditures (over social programs), and disproportionate economic growth has led to the feminization of poverty and has especially impacted women in low-income nations not only economically but also socially and culturally. Such recognitions are undoubtedly valuable, because the platform connects women's poverty to local and national political and historical power structures—not individual women's personal circumstances or their personal behavior, as subsequent initiatives do. In other words, the Beijing Platform highlights the vectors of subjugation that impact women and thereby provides a *holistic* and *contextual* account of how gender might be mainstreamed at all levels of policy, including how its final material outcomes affect women's (and men's) lived experiences.

As a result of the Fourth World Conference on Women, supranational organizations such as the United Nations and the World Bank, national governments, and even aid organizations made serious attempts to reconceptualize their development agendas with the intention that they would follow the Beijing Platform. Many institutions publicly sought to promote an "active and visible policy of mainstreaming a gender perspective into all policies and programmes" so that they analyze "the effects on women and men, respectively" (*Beijing Declaration* 27). However, these gender mainstreaming initiatives looked very different from the sorts of projects that the Beijing Platform may have intended. The subsequent gender mainstreaming policies and programs in no way reflected the Beijing Platform, despite the platform's very clear and dynamic definition of gender mainstreaming, its nuanced understanding of the need to address issues of gender inequality in regards to social programs, development practices, and neocolonial power relations, *and* despite global policy makers vocal and public support for gender mainstreaming initiatives. The variety of ways in which gender mainstreaming rhetorics function in documents post Beijing demonstrates the need to look at how rhetorics travel and how, as they do, they shift, change, and are redefined.[2]

The United States, for example, actively supported gender mainstreaming initiatives at the Beijing conference, but shortly thereafter, Congress passed the Personal Responsibility and Work Opportunity Reconciliation Act of 1996, which focused on mainstreaming poor women by regulating their behaviors and their role in the U.S. economy. The very title of the act, and the policy's overwhelming focus on women, demonstrates how gender mainstreaming ideologies conjoin with a rhetoric of personal responsibility, thereby shifting the definition of mainstreaming away from a vectored and holistic definition and instead toward a focus on individual behavior (part of the focus of chapter 2). Indeed, the policy's emphasis on work and personal responsibility already clearly decontextualizes women's poverty by *not* drawing attention to, for example, the long-standing ties between poverty and racism or how ten years of deindustrialization in the United States had caused a drop in middle-class incomes and a corresponding rise in service sector jobs that do not provide benefits for women. So although the United States supported the notion of gender mainstreaming, the first lines of the Personal Responsibility Act reflect the ways in which the United States translated gender mainstreaming imperatives into a rhetoric of personal responsibility: "The

Congress makes the following findings: (1) Marriage is the foundation to a successful society" (Personal Responsibility and Work Opportunity Reconciliation Act of 1996 101[1]) and through the support of marriage women ought to "transition from economic dependency [on the State] to self-sufficiency through work" (817[c]). In short, the Personal Responsibility Act argues that to prepare women for a postindustrial, neoliberal economy, the policy must attempt to make women responsible caregivers *inside* the home through the institution of marriage and more productive workers *outside* the home through paid labor. Employing the rhetoric of rational choice economics and focusing on teaching women to make what the policy portrays as "better" choices, this neoliberal policy also drastically cut traditional safety-net benefits, housing and childcare allowances, education programs, unemployment assistance, and even disability subsidies in the name of "personal responsibility" (Jaggar 299).

This kind of rhetoric of personal responsibility within the context of gender mainstreaming can also be traced further beyond the U.S. borders where the rhetoric of gender mainstreaming shifts again and connects with notions of economic fitness (the focus of chapter 3). In 1997, just two years after the Beijing conference and very much in response to the Beijing Platform's gender mainstreaming initiative, the World Bank, the largest and most powerful global development agency, publicly announced that women are the keys to a nation's economic success. In a speech called "The Challenge of Inclusion," which I explore further in chapter 2, given by then World Bank president James Wolfensohn, he stated that it was time for the World Bank to make a formal commitment to include women in the "mainstream" of global development. Wolfensohn used this speech to argue that it was time for the Bank and development experts to mainstream gender and women's place in the development process; it was time, he concluded, to "include" women and bring "into society [those people] who have never been part of it before" (1–2). Significantly, Wolfensohn went on to define the "challenge of inclusion" as "bringing more and more people into the economic mainstream" (3) in order to "make the unfit fit" (5). In this example, Wolfensohn successfully connects the notion of gender mainstreaming to the notion of fitness—not only economic fitness but, given that he speaks about women from so-called developing nations, fitness defined by global capitalism. In other words, Wolfensohn attaches the rhetoric of gender mainstreaming to eugenicist and colonial aims thereby divorcing the notion of gender mainstreaming from the dynamic meaning put forth by the Beijing Platform (a topic I explore further in chapter 3).

By tracing how gender mainstreaming rhetorics circulate within various policies and how they are networked with new and sometimes conflicting ideologies, we can see how rhetorical meaning is not always stable. Rhetorics can shift and, thus, have drastically different material effects. As John Trimbur has made clear, the circulation of rhetorics and writing cannot be isolated from the material conditions that make that circulation possible (190). For example, further working directly against the recommendations of the Beijing Platform, which stressed the need to consider how women's poverty relates to broader social, political, and economic conditions, post–Beijing World Bank loan parameters and International Monetary Fund currency devaluation initiatives reduced the very social programs designed to help women succeed in the paid labor market (Rittich 249)—programs that the platform notes are key to helping women achieve empowerment.

By briefly demonstrating how arguments for gender mainstreaming are networked across several documents, we can see how, just after the Fourth World International Conference on Women and the subsequent rise of strong global support for public policies that included gender mainstreaming imperatives, policy makers certainly did focus on *women,* but they specifically focused on their behavior and individual abilities to be core economic actors for their families and communities. In addition, by networking these policy arguments we can note that while the public rhetoric of gender mainstreaming is supposedly constant, *meaning* and rhetorical purpose change as it moves from policy to policy, from supranation to nation.

In other words, the above transnational feminist rhetorical analysis illustrates that the rhetoric of gender mainstreaming ultimately becomes attached to acontextual rhetorics of self-determination, responsibility, family values, and tradition. What appears to be a common rhetoric of "gender mainstreaming" is not actually common at all. While gender mainstreaming within the context of the Beijing Platform is intended to create policy and development initiatives that address the wide context of women's inequality, in practice gender mainstreaming projects set into motion several successive development programs and policies that employed rhetorics of personal responsibility, economic fitness, and empowerment as a way to mainstream women into the global economy; yet these policies remarkably end up reinforcing gender and global inequalities. These rhetorical variations make it necessary for rhetoricians to look carefully at policymaking practices through the lens of transnational networks so that we can identify the multiple strands of influence that give a policy argument clout and demonstrate how repetitive lore often circulates on a transglocal scale, blending the local and global across national or political boundaries (Dingo and Scott).

To answer Anna Lowenhaupt Tsing's question, which is the epigraph to this chapter, about how we might study global connections, I offer a transnational feminist rhetorical methodology that seeks to identify how arguments are networked, how and why rhetorics travel and circulate, and then how (due to rhetorical occasions such as the rise of neoliberal economics)[3] they shift and change as they move across geopolitical boundaries to reflect different ideas about production, labor, and global citizenship. The way in which policy makers address women's role in an increasing neoliberal and global economy should be of crucial concern for feminist rhetoricians because, as I argue, although topoi like gender mainstreaming appear to have a universal definition, meaning shifts as topoi transverse geopolitical contexts and exist within different policies. The circulation of the term *gender mainstreaming* that I have analyzed above shows how and why the practice of feminist rhetorical analysis must be brought to bear on public policy, globalization, and the transnational movement of texts and ideas. Feminist rhetoricians must consider how policy rhetorics are linked—how they are disseminated, received, rewritten, and put into action—in unexpected ways. The goal of *Networking Arguments*, then, is first to demonstrate a new method of feminist rhetorical analysis that pays attention to how rhetorics are networked and travel, thereby moving the public toward a better understanding of the uneven impact of globalization on women, and, second, to enact this method by tracing three central terms that circulate within late twentieth-century global gender policies and initiatives—mainstreaming, fitness, and empowerment—in order to show how, as they travel, their meanings shift and change depending upon the contexts in which policy makers and development experts use them. Ultimately, by turning to transnational feminist theory, feminist rhetoricians can learn how to network arguments so that they might gauge the various and shifting representational and material effects of globalization on women.

WHY TRANSNATIONAL FEMINIST STUDIES?

Contemporary globalization (through the proliferation of international trade agreements and policies, transnational corporations, and migration alongside new and efficient communication networks) has enabled economic, social, political, and cultural connectivities between and among nations and thus has also affected the ways in which texts are produced, circulated, and used. These connectivities have inspired scholars across disciplines to think in new ways, not only about international politics but also about how contemporary globalization has made it necessary to examine the flow of ideas, goods, people, and texts across borders (see Levitt and Khagram). Globalization, specifically subsequent changes to national economies, has had an uneven impact on women across the globe; for example, at the end of the twentieth century and the beginning of the twenty-first century there has been a rise in women's poverty worldwide in addition to women increasingly migrating (often without their family members) to other countries for work (*2004 World Survey* 9). Thus, to further answer Tsing's opening epigraph question—how should we study global connections—requires new feminist rhetorical methods and theories that pay attention to the transnational networked relationships and connections among texts within the frameworks of globalization and the rise of neoliberal and neocolonial practices.

The term *transnational*, while defined in a number of ways, generally refers to how globalization has influenced the movement of people and the production of texts, culture, and knowledge across borders so that the strict distinctions among nations and national practices can become blurred.[4] In the last ten years, disciplines throughout the humanities and social sciences have recognized that increasing globalization and enduring neoliberal economics have changed our understandings of citizenship, place, and texts. Drawing heavily from the fields of political science, sociology, geography, and women's studies, the emergent interdisciplinary field of transnational studies has sought to "uncover, analyze, and conceptualize similarities, differences, and interactions among trans-societal and trans-organizational realities, including the ways in which they shape bordered and bounded phenomena and dynamics across time and space" (Levitt and Khagram 10–11).[5] Transnational feminists add a political edge to this study of globalization by tracing how increasing global capitalism can create conditions of economic exploitation for some women and possibilities for others. Transnational feminists also draw important attention to the relationship between neoliberal economics and neoliberal governmentality (see Brown) citing how, at the end of the twentieth century, neoliberalism inundated not only the global economy but cultural practices as well. Generally neoliberal polices have been critiqued by feminists for being indifferent to poverty, social development, and environmental destruction (Brown 18). In this way, then neoliberalism functions on several scales: policy, economy, and culture. The political economist Susan George characterizes the neoliberal economy in the following way: "the State . . . reduce[s] its role in the economy, . . . and citizens [are] given much less rather than much more social protection" (27). Anthony Giddens, likewise, notes that neoliberal policies are "link[ed to supporting] unfettered market forces [and] to a defense of traditional institutions, particularly the family and nation" (12).

Thus, the rise of neoliberalism is an important historical and ideological touch point for this book. Roughly defined, the term *neoliberalism* has come to describe the economic philosophy that markets will always regulate themselves and thus that governments and policy makers ought to promote free market capitalism and strategies such as global trade and the development of global markets so that goods may flow freely between nations with few to no regulations, including taxes and tariffs (see Steger and Roy).[6]

Historically, the term first appeared post–World War II via economic and legal scholars associated with the Freiburgh School in Germany. They used the term to refer to revivifying classical liberalism. Throughout the 1970s and '80s Latin American economists adopted this revivified term to support their pro-market model of development. Later in the 1990s, activists and scholars embraced neoliberalism as a pejorative term that describes the pro-market, American-style capitalism that is associated with the Washington Consensus—a set of economic development policies for the Global South supported by the U.S. government, the World Bank, and the International Monetary Fund (ix–x).

Today neoliberalism is a common term that refers not only to market-centric policies, free trade, and the spread of global capitalism but also to how individuals ought to act. In other words, the *ideology* of neoliberalism trickles into our everyday lived experiences (see Riedner and Mahoney) and manifests within particular values: entrepreneurship, competition, individual choice, self-interest, and self-empowerment. As Manfred B. Steger and Ravi Roy aptly state: neoliberalism "puts the production and exchange of material goods at the heart of the human experience" (12). Neoliberal policies then extend capitalist market logic—that is, competition, free trade, and business—to all institutions, including social welfare. Wendy Brown illustrates that neoliberalism has turned into a form of "political rationality" that extends beyond market economics to the management (and then self-management) of people. As I explore further in chapter 2, neoliberal governmentality, which embraces rational choice economics, works at the level of the individual and thus produces neoliberal actors. Neoliberalism is often articulated through a rhetoric of choice (consumer, personal, behavior, and so on). Moreover, neoliberal policies also went into effect alongside the rise of multiculturalism in the United States and elsewhere, creating rhetorics that stripped notions of equality, difference, and equity away from their structural causes (see Duggan). In this way, as Inderpal Grewal notes, neoliberal policies have also managed to at once rearticulate colonial histories and feminist goals together (15). As Grewal maintains, "neoliberalism produces its own geopolitics in terms of how market logics could be linked to social concerns for differently located, gendered, and racialized populations" (19).

Thus transnational feminists tend to trace the economic, social, and political conditions of contemporary neoliberalism, neocolonialism, and neoimperialism across nations, asking how these sorts of practices link diverse nations and people and shape them in similar and different ways. In addition, transnational feminists examine the roles that state and supranational power, history, class relations, and sexual, gendered, raced, and ethnic expectations play in the making and unmaking of nations and nation-states and the movement of goods, ideas, and people across and within borders.

Feminist scholars such as Grewal, Caren Kaplan, Nancy Naples, Chandra Mohanty, and Valentine Moghadam have suggested that globalization has had uneven material consequences throughout and within different regions of the world, making it necessary to employ a transnational feminist lens to consider the vectors of power (often present within textual production through representational practices) that impact categories of identity, state sovereignty, and the markers of citizenship. According to Shari Stone-Mediatore, "transnational feminists situate language practices within far-reaching political and economic systems," (129) including global to local relations, as well as state-to-state and supranational transactions. Transnational feminist scholars seek to examine "'transnational social spaces,' or linkages among political actors across borders" (Moghadam 81), and in so doing, they use the metaphor of networks and connectivity to describe uneven transnational power relationships and their impact on women. This transnational feminist network model emphasizes that the identity category of "woman" is entangled within a variety of connections (Grewal 24),[7] and to understand women's oppression, feminists must consider not only a woman's local circumstance but how her circumstances *relate to* and are *informed by* supranational policies, colonial history, global economic structures, and even our practices here in the West—the very vectors of power that the Beijing Platform emphasizes.

For transnational feminists, then, networking is a useful metaphor because it draws attention to the links between women's diverse experiences, aspirations, and identities. For instance, a transnational feminist lens notes women's material realities by seeing the economic, political, class, and gendered connections between Mexican maquiladora workers (i.e., female factory workers along the Mexican-U.S. border) and U.S. megastore workers. Due to trade agreements such as the North American Free Trade Agreement of 1995 (NAFTA), maquiladora workers may now be making the very same products that U.S. middle-class workers were making over a decade ago but for significantly reduced wages. U.S. workers may face unemployment and growing debts due to a lack of the job security that factory jobs may have formerly provided. While these same U.S. workers also might be able to sustain some portion of their pre-NAFTA lifestyle because the low wages maquiladora workers make enable U.S. companies to keep the cost of products down, these same U.S. workers may now also work in low-paying blue-collar jobs that do not provide benefits, childcare, or vacation. Thus, like their maquiladora-working counterparts, U.S. workers may struggle to make ends meet. Both the maquiladora and U.S. workers' economic situation may be linked by an international trade agreement, by the products one produces and the other sells (and/or can or cannot purchase), and the fact that both are not thriving in this transnational economy. Simply comparing these two groups of people's economic statuses does not elucidate the complex ways in which they are linked by a transnational economy. A transnational feminist analysis does not simply recover lost voices nor does it ask who suffers more or how two (or more) groups are similar; instead, transnational feminism illustrate a matrix of connections between people, nations, economies, and the textual practices present in, for example, public policies and popular culture.

Just as transnational feminists have begun to query the ways in which globalization must shift how feminists think about gender identity, power, and the connections between the local and global, the field of feminist rhetorical studies has been predominantly concerned with the historical effort to recover and recognize the spaces of women's rhetorical practices by mapping oppression or hierarchical structures based on race, class, gender, sexuality, and ability. The field has worked to widen the scope of how we define women's rhetorical practices. In May 2006, however, Wendy S. Hesford made a call to the field of feminist rhetorical studies to address globalization. Drawing on atrocities at Abu Graib, Hesford notes that rhetoric and composition scholars need to create methods and frameworks that not only move the public toward a better understanding of the uneven impact of globalization but also move them toward fostering social justice. As Hesford makes clear, composition and rhetoric scholars have had a strong interest in factoring globalization's impact into their scholarly work. Yet, while the scholarship on globalization tends to weave through some specific areas of rhetoric and composition studies (Hesford traces, for example, rhetoric and composition studies' focus on "unidirectional English monolingualism" [789], ethnography, composition pedagogy, and rhetorical history), there have been few sustained studies in the field organized around how rhetoric and composition studies scholars must extend their methods of analysis to consider the transnational movement of texts, specifically. For this reason Hesford ultimately invites rhetoric and composition scholars to study the formation of transnational publics by considering the "intertextuality of local and global cultures," tracing the global networks and paths on which texts circulate, and reframing how we read and attend to the local (792).[8] This gap demonstrates the necessity for a transnational feminist rhetorical analytic that explores the relationship between language and power and considers how power works in specific historical moments and within specific texts. Because feminist rhetorical scholars are uniquely situated to study how globalization affects how we write, read, and are persuaded across and within the boundaries of the nation-state, they should have a vested interest in widening the scope of feminist rhetorical study to include transnational feminist theory. But what does that look like?

Hesford, in her call for the field of rhetorical studies to address globalization and the transnational movement of texts, suggests that rhetorical theorists often "take for granted the nation-state and citizen-subject as units of analysis" (788). Likewise, Eileen Schell notes that traditional rhetorical study assumes that "a rhetor speaks or writes from a particular location in time and space to a particular audience" (168). Yet Schell continues by explaining that globalization necessitates that rhetoricians "account for . . . how national interests and appeals are tied up in complex international and transnational flows of capital and people" (168). Both Hesford and Schell call for rhetorical scholars to incorporate into their research methods a transnational perspective that examines how economic globalization has influenced both the flow of knowledge and rhetorics across international borders while also paying attention not only to individual speech acts or occasion-bound rhetorics but the circulation of arguments about women.

This very sentiment is also noted by transnational feminist theorist J. K. Gibson-Graham,[9] who claims that, due to the rise of contemporary globalization and the transnational movement of goods and texts, "the vision of feminist politics as grounded in persons [needs to be] extended . . . to include another ontological substrate: a vast set of disarticulated 'places' . . . connected through webs of signification" (xxiv). For Gibson-Graham, feminist analysis should not be just about the "category 'woman' or identity" (xxiv); rather, they suggest feminists must examine how women are part of and affected by a complex network of relationships. This means that feminist rhetoricians must critically examine arguments about women within the context of globalization by considering how rhetorical arguments about them become layered and connected to other information, *and* they must also trace how rhetorics shift and change as they travel.

The network model thus provides an effective way for feminist rhetoricians to think through transnational power relationships, especially in light of how rhetorics travel and are dispersed across the globe and how the circulation of rhetorics impacts representations of women and women's material well-being and their abilities to speak and be heard (Grewal 2). For feminist rhetoricians then, engaging a transnational feminist rhetorical analysis means examining the "variety of sites" whereby "subjects [women, men, children] become constituted and connected" (Grewal 23) and texts "in *relational* terms," paying attention to "different, often conflictual, locations and histories" (Mohanty qtd. in Bahri 75).

So, for example, returning to my introductory example of gender mainstreaming, if we only examined occasion-bound and individual-bound rhetorical acts without tracing the resulting policies and program initiatives that emerged within the context of the global support for gender mainstreaming, then we might have ignored their diverse material impact on women. However, as we place a transnational feminist rhetorical lens on the aforementioned example, we see how policy makers' assumptions about poor and Third World women drive the creation and implementation of contemporary global economic policies. Thus, we see how crucial it is to bring a transnational lens to a feminist rhetorical analysis in order to look beyond individual texts or occasions and instead examine how rhetorics relate to each other, the time in which they are produced, and how they are employed.

I propose adopting a transnational feminist rhetorical analytic that not only examines rhetorical acts as they relate to identity categories or historical moments but also engages how complex networks of relationships affect rhetorical meaning. Globalization and the transnational movement of texts not only makes it necessary for us to consider how global forces shape lives and literate practices (Hesford) but also how such forces make it necessary for rhetorical scholars to examine the circulations of rhetorics transnationally. This method might be derived from transnational feminist theory, which considers how representational practices are affected by social, political, cultural, and economic forces that are interconnected. This approach to rhetorical analysis also (and importantly) grounds transnational feminist theory by analyzing and making connections between specific rhetorics about women that are produced throughout disparate locations and texts. I contend that such a rhetorical methodology more effectively illustrates how transnational rhetorical acts and representations are often the results of a colonial understanding of difference, imperialist aims, and/or a neoliberal philosophy of personal achievement. Ultimately, a transnational feminist rhetorical analytic is necessary to show how these rhetorical acts relate to one another and how they shift and change as they cross national and developmental boundaries.

NETWORKING ARGUMENTS: A TRANSNATIONAL FEMINIST RHETORICAL THEORY

For feminist rhetoricians to study global connections requires new methods and theories that pay attention to the transnational networked relationships among texts within the frameworks of globalization and the rise of neoliberal and neocolonial practices. Scholars of transnationalism suggest that increased telecommunications and computer networks as well as a growing global economy and immigration have made it necessary for scholars to examine the flow of ideas, goods, people, and texts across borders (see Levitt and Khagram). However, for rhetoricians, this flow calls into question the situatedness of texts and the traditional rhetorical relationship of text, speaker, and audience and demonstrates the need to look at how rhetorics circulate and how that circulation relates to (geo)political economies.

Thus, feminist rhetoricians must not only examine occasion- or nation-bound rhetorics but also how arguments are transnationally networked and how neoliberal economics and neocolonial power relationships are often exigencies for particular arguments and representations of women, their needs, and their place in the global economy. These exigencies, coupled with Hesford and Schell's recognition of looking at rhetorical acts outside of the bounded nation-state and citizen-subject, necessitate that rhetoricians find new ways to examine how texts are written, dispersed, and circulated, how they persuade, and how they might impact audiences who reside in very different geopolitical locations. The metaphor of the network is an effective way for thinking through both how discourses travel, circulate, and are dispersed across the globe (Grewal 23) and how transnational power relationships impact these representational practices; it helps rhetoricians to establish associations among texts, while also showing "how ideas [and rhetorics] fluctuate in specific types of spaces and contexts" (Rice 131).

Tracing the circulation of rhetorics across transnational networks, however, complicates rhetorical study because this movement challenges the "homeostatic relationship" (Edbauer 9) between audience, text, and writer or speaker. As the transnational feminist Grewal explains, transnational "circulations, productions, and consumptions cannot be understood as a demarcated 'local' realm of action, but rather as . . . caught up within the movement of people, goods, and ideas across national boundaries, . . . produc[ing] . . . gendered subjects" (28). Grewal's ideas resound with rhetorical scholars such as Jenny Edbauer who draws attention to the importance of looking at rhetorical acts outside of a static rhetorical situation. Although not in the context of globalization or the transnational movement of texts, theorists such as Lloyd Bitzer have considered how rhetorical exigencies and external contexts can shape a rhetorical act. More recently, Edbauer has further complicated Bitzer's argument by showing how rhetorical acts relate to what Edbauer describes as "the operation of . . . links and circulation" (7). Edbauer, pointing to the work of Craig Smith and Scott Lybarger, suggests that "rhetorical communication is always in a state of flux" (Smith and Lybarger qtd. in Edbauer 8), making it necessary for rhetoricians to consider how, as rhetorics circulate, they are influenced by "connections" that ultimately change rhetorical meaning (Edbauer 12). To this extent, Edbauer also extends John Trimbur's recognition that "the circuits of production, distribution, exchange, and consumption through which [rhetoric] circulates" impact how rhetorics take on "cultural value and worldly force[s]" (194). As Trimbur makes clear, rhetorical production and circulation *cannot* be separated from the political economy or the material conditions of writing. Contemporary globalization has enabled the circulation of texts across national borders and as such makes it necessary to further trouble the contained relationship between the writer or speaker, audience, and text by illuminating how rhetorical "action [can be] dislocated [or] delegated" (Latour 166) so that there might not now be *a* specific actor, speaker, or writer, nor a specific audience.

Furthering the aforementioned scholars' arguments about the importance of looking at the circulation of arguments as they relate to the political economy, then, women, and their rhetorical acts, can no longer serve as the only central objects of study; rather, women (and discourses about women) must be recognized as part of a *network* of relationships that affect how women's identities are represented in various situations. Thus, to network arguments, feminist rhetoricians must not only consider the places where rhetorics travel and are deployed but also the external social, economic, and political influences that serve as exigencies for particular policy arguments about women. Unlike the work done by rhetorical scholars such as Bitzer and Edbauer,[10] when feminist rhetoricians network arguments they draw attention to power relations as well as the political and material consequences of rhetorical circulation.[11]

The metaphor of the network is employed here because it provides a plausible method of examining texts through the lenses of transnationalism and rhetoric. This metaphor allows rhetoricians to consider how the rise of neoliberal economics, neocolonial power relationships, and the permeability of nation-state borders create "new forms of communication" that are comprised of networks of logics shared between nations (True and Mintrom 28). These networks are not just figurative but are made possible by the expansion, power, and knowledge exchanges among supranational organizations such as the World Bank, International Monetary Fund, transnational corporations, and nation-states. Jacqui True and Michael Mintrom argue that "transnational networks serve as conduits . . . of information about differing policy initiatives" (28). Grewal adds that "transnational connectivities" along the network's web always follow "historicized trajectories" (22). Grewal and True and Mintrom envision networks as webs of connections and linkages; we might imagine that nation-states, NGOs, supranational agencies, and their resulting policies are conduits on the network that transmit particular ideologies throughout the network's web.

The network contains a collection of nodes representing the concentration of power of some countries and organizations and the limitations of it in others—some portions of this network may be dense and clustered, others more dispersed. This network, as Grewal points out, may move rhetorics from one node of power to another, some "get translated and transcoded," others are "unevenly connected, [and still] others are strongly connected" (23). This nuanced network model accounts for material, rhetorical, cultural, and economic linkages among nations and revises the familiar hierarchical top-down model of economic development wherein one nation controls, has power over, and directly influences another—a more linear model of globalization that does not account for the back and forth and indeed far dispersion of arguments.

The network model shows how power is distributed and concentrated in some areas, how that power connects to and reaches other nations, and how these nations are inextricably linked to each other. Following Grewal, then, I offer the metaphor of the network to think about the connectivities that reframe commonplace rhetorics. In this model, power is not something agents have or do not have, instead that power is relational. This network model offers a new way of looking at rhetorical agency and power that is much more complex.

By networking arguments, rhetoricians can demonstrate the complex ways that rhetorical appeals reach a diffused yet linked audience while also accounting for how contiguous power relationships add meaning and force to arguments. Such an approach enables feminist rhetoricians to better decipher the rhetorical and material impact of arguments while also emphasizing how women, in what are often called the First and Third Worlds, are linked. So, for example, the above described call to mainstream a gender perspective into policy turned into policies that seek to promote personal responsibility, to train women (as Wolfensohn so eloquently stated) to fit into global economy, and to empower women to be entrepreneurs—all of which are part of the transnational neoliberal rhetoric that this book traces. In other words, to understand policy arguments, rhetoricians must consider the circulating rhetorics that link domestic institutional change with emerging international norms and vice versa. Networking arguments enables feminist rhetoricians to expose how domestic and international policies are transnationally and rhetorically linked through complex neoliberal and gendered ideologies and how the commonplace terms that circulate within these policies are dependent upon each other.

When scholars ignore the subtleties and circulation of rhetorics, especially as they pass from one location to another, they do not account for how transnational practices, ideas, or texts are not homeostatic or sacrosanct but rhetorical—the topos mainstreaming, for example, may look similar across a variety of texts, but as the term circulates, it ultimately engages different arguments, carries different meanings, and has distinct material effects depending on context and location (McRuer 11). As we saw above, gender mainstreaming policies may focus on women as economic actors but ultimately each policy makes very different arguments under the topos of "mainstreaming." While reading for dominance is clearly important work, a transnational feminist analysis highlights that at the very least dominance *looks* different depending on an audience member's context or location. Gender mainstreaming practices, therefore, cannot be deemed as inherently good or bad; rather, to understand the rhetoric of gender mainstreaming we must consider how meanings shift and change due to context, history, and even intention. In other words, these rhetorics are part of a network of transnational relationships that enable them to slip from and be repurposed for one context or another.

To reiterate the importance of examining how arguments are networked, the World Bank's implementation of gender mainstreaming policies, alongside the simultaneous global decline of the welfare state, is an example of inextricably linked yet competing and incongruous logic. U.S. welfare policies and World Bank gender mainstreaming policies both concentrate on making women materially responsible for their families' own economic situation; however, the U.S. Personal Responsibility Act urges single mothers to marry while several gender mainstreaming World Bank policies attempt to deemphasize Third World women's "traditional" familial relationships and in doing so encourage them to work outside the home as a form of liberation from traditional roles. Women from the Global South are stereotypically characterized as those in need of emancipation by the First World from oppressive gender cultural norms. In contrast, U.S. women tend to be represented as free, autonomous, and liberated subjects unattached to patriarchal structures. These policy depictions may appear to be paradoxical, but both sets of policies characterize poor women as backwards or, in the words of Wolfensohn, "unfit." The Personal Responsibility Act represents women as needing to be more integrated into patriarchal structures by becoming proper mothers and wives in a capitalist economy, at once caring and accountable wife-mothers and responsible and productive workers. World Bank policies (as I explore further in subsequent chapters), in contrast, recommend that Third World women be taught to be capitalist entrepreneurs who are economically independent of their family, husbands, and sometimes even their community.

Despite these differences, these public policy arguments link First and Third World women by portraying women simultaneously as individual earners and producers for the global economy. World Bank gender mainstreaming policies and U.S. welfare policies contain appeals to traditional liberal ideologies of rights, choice, and individual agency. Both policy arguments rhetorically and materially interpolate women within a capitalist economy—a system reliant upon class and, in this case, gender stratification. The grand narrative of mainstreaming attempts to change women's behavior and shift women's dependency from the state to the market (and ultimately to the global capitalist economy) while heightening gender stratification by making women primarily responsible for their poor families. Although achieved through slightly different ideals, U.S. welfare policies and the World Bank's gender mainstreaming policies share a common rhetoric, which suggests that material inequalities can be overcome by managing women's actions. Understanding this networked relationship enables rhetoricians to examine how contemporary policy arguments are attached to historical relationships of power and how these arguments get reinterpreted and rewritten during economic shifts such as the rise of neoliberalism.

The practice of networking arguments can also expand the work of transnational feminists by connecting the ways in which patterns of persuasion are affected by extra-rhetorical forces, such as the rise of transnational capital, enduring (neo)colonial relationships, and neoliberalism, to create policies that attempt to address women's role in an expanding global economy. Ultimately, through this wide-angle view, feminist rhetoricians (and transnational feminists) can start to uncover the myriad arguments that institutions employ to address women's social, economic, and cultural needs and better understand how these arguments (and their intended solutions) often play a part in women's disenfranchisement or their empowerment.

Networking Arguments demonstrates a transnational feminist rhetorical analysis by considering the transnational paths along which rhetorics travel. I offer not only another instance of how rhetoric "works" to persuade, showing how arguments operate in public policy and result in specific material effects, but I also illustrate how emerging transnational meanings shift as they travel along complex policy networks. I turn to public policies concerning women's place in the global economy, like the ones I briefly analyze above, as examples of the specific sites where we can trace the common and sometimes uneven impact of transnationalism. I place policy texts within a network in order to show how a complex set of relationships impacts the arguments each policy makes. Part of the work of the rhetorical critic then is to look beyond shared commonplaces and illuminate the various ways arguments are collected, composed, *and* assembled.

WHY A TRANSNATIONAL FEMINIST RHETORICAL ANALYSIS OF PUBLIC POLICY?

Public policy analysis is generally defined as "the systematic investigation of alternative policy options and the assembly and integration of the evidence for and against each option" (Ukeles 223). Typical policy analysis takes a problem-solving approach and uses statistical data to predict the best course of action a policy should take next. This sort of policy analysis takes into account a policy's design, implementation, and whether the policy has met its stated goal or not. Some forms of policy analysis may factor a specific point of view into their analysis; for example, the World Bank uses a specific "gender responsive social analysis" to consider how the Bank's policies attend to women's needs (poverty reduction, infant mortality, availability of paid labor, etc.) (Kvam). While there are several models of policy analysis, most models are prescriptive and tend to use quantitative methods that emphasize economic and political influences and outcomes. These prescriptive sorts of studies may examine the history of how a policy issue has come about and/or how it was written in order to learn from past policy mistakes, but these studies rarely make connections between other policy decisions, nor do they account for larger contextual issues that might influence how or why a policy is written. In fact, most models for policy making and analysis follow a closed system that begins with identifying a problem, documenting its effects, creating a responsive policy, gathering feedback about the policy (this might take place through testimonies, debates, or policy analysis), rewriting the policy, and then implementing the policy (see Nelson). Final policies are essentially written through the circulation of rhetorics. Traditional policy analysis does not network arguments; it does not account for rhetorical circulation or the ways that lore, stereotypes, economic agendas, global affairs, transnational business practices, and history, for example, impact policy decisions and implementation, nor does it account for how policy functions rhetorically.

Yet, public policies are intrinsically rhetorical;[12] at the very least, the testimonies and hearings that are the cornerstone of policy making reflects Quintilian's *vir bonus* definition of rhetoric as enacted or embodied by the "good man speaking well." But a transnational feminist rhetorical analysis of public policy making must look beyond how individual people might persuade an audience. As Nancy Welch has suggested, a rhetorical analysis of public policy can help uncover how certain arguments are vulnerable to co-optation or appropriation (384). Extending Welch's observation, I argue that a transnational feminist rhetorical analysis of public policy can demonstrate the ways in which history and local and global contexts impact why and how a policy is written, consider how policy makers' history, culture, and conceptual framework informs policy writing, and reveal the multiple motives behind policy making. It is difficult to discern who is the key writer of an actual policy (for example, the Beijing Platform for Action was written at the conference and its final version contains the authorial revisions of several people across a span of time and across geopolitical locale). Likewise, because global policy arguments are not bound to the nation-state and instead cross national and developmental boundaries, to understand a policy's rhetorical situation rhetoricians must place them in a transnational, networked lens.

To analyze public policy rhetorically is to analyze transnational networks; public policy is not just another text upon which we might perform a rhetorical analysis. Rather, because policy making is a dynamic and dialectic process, to examine only the final policy text tells us little about the policy's rhetoricity; a singular policy does not contain *a* speaker, *a* writer, or *an* audience. Policies are assemblages of "interactions distributed elsewhere in time and space" (Latour 194). While clearly, texts have speakers and writers, Bruno Latour describes how arguments are often deployed unselfconsciously so that the "source of initiative" (216) is often unclear. Likewise, Hesford echoes Ellen Gorsevski's point that globalization produces a unique "rhetorical climate" that is an "intersubjective and interactional phenomenon" (Hesford, "Global Turns" 794) where "there is not a discrete rhetor and audience or singular material text; all are mutually influential to the point of being indistinguishable" (Gorsevski qtd. in Hesford, "Global Turns" 794). Latour's and Gorsevski's observations are particularly useful for understanding public policy's unique rhetorical situation. As noted by Andrea Lunsford and Lisa Ede (and later J. Blake Scott), sometimes the "audience addressed" and "audience invoked" in texts—and especially in transnational policy texts—by policy makers is an ever-present yet intangible wider audience of citizens at-large and a more immediate audience of fellow policy makers. Thus, to analyze public policy rhetorically, scholars have worked to widen their analytic scope.[13]

Public policy, then, further complicates this relationship since the actor, the writer, or the speaker is not one person or entity. For example, when U.S. legislation is signed into law, the text itself has been touched by testimonies, committees, mark ups, and amendments as well as by the present economic climate, presidential acceptance ratings, "wars on terror," levels of security, global trade circuits, and historical representations, to name only a few, to the point that naming *an actor* or *writer* becomes impossible.[14] Likewise, policy-guiding documents produced for UN conferences are written over a course of time, and these documents are influenced by nation-state financial support, donors, and conflicting members of UN committees (for example, often feminist organizations and the Vatican both sit on the same UN committees and thus must compromise their values to conceive a workable policy initiative).

A transnational feminist rhetorical lens on public policy, specifically, will help reveal how the movement of people and the production of texts, culture, and knowledge across borders and political, social, and economic forces impacts how policy makers craft their arguments. Moreover, a transnational rhetorical feminist analysis of public policy will help us better attend to the uneven impacts of globalization and help us see how topoi and their attached arguments circulate and then are reframed for differing purposes. In other words, a network of transnational relationships enables rhetorics to slip from and be repurposed for one context or another.

Public policy thus offers rhetoricians a rich site for examining how globalization and transnational relationships affect how we write, read, and are persuaded across the borders of the nation-state. I turn to late twentieth-century policies that address women's needs in particular because, as I mention above, at the end of the twentieth century global economic shifts made it necessary for policy makers to rethink the role of the state and its relationship to citizens and reconsider how citizens might thrive in this new economy. In particular, I consider how at the end of the twentieth century neoliberal ideologies inundated the global economy. As Grewal notes, neoliberal policies have also managed to at once rearticulate colonial histories and feminist goals together (15). The changes to welfare programs and policies across the globe, for example, might have been in the name of "gender mainstreaming," but they reflect transnational neoliberal logics and demonstrate networked policy arguments that reimagine identity, family, and economic citizenship for this new economy. Yet, neoliberalism has had an uneven impact across the globe, strengthening state power in some locations and significantly diminishing it in others (Grewal 16).[15] As Grewal maintains, "neoliberalism produces its own geopolitics in terms of how market logics could be linked to social concerns for differently located, gendered, and racialized populations"; thus, it is important for transnational feminist rhetorical studies to consider neoliberalism (19). Networking arguments, then, means not only looking at how rhetorics travel but also looking at how, within individual policies, there are vectors of power (i.e., colonial history, supranational relationships, economic plans, gendered assumptions, etc.) that we need to unpack to understand the cultural (i.e., how neoliberalism structures our intimate lives) and material (i.e., how it impacts our economic well-being) work that the policy does.

In *Networking Arguments*, I trace the networked relationships among several policies that impact gendered relationships and that center around common terms that have emerged during the height of contemporary globalization. I consider the historical moments, social actors, and cultural memories that inform how policy texts are written and when they contain commonplace vocabularies yet vastly different arguments. Public policy is not written in one place—a final policy is merely a tangible outcome of a set of distributed logics that are boundless: legal rule, personal experience, cultural memories, history, political ideologies, economic relationships, transnational connectivities.

Therefore, feminist rhetoricians must examine the arguments of many pieces and parts that inform policy texts. My book's analysis demonstrates how, due to globalization and increasing transnational connectivities, we might for a moment set aside our traditional understanding of audience, text, and author and instead examine how history, relationships, connections, and contexts impact the persuasiveness, pervasiveness, and contradictions of certain arguments that circulate globally at the end of the twentieth century.

NETWORKING POLICY COMMONPLACES

The policies that I examine in this book provide examples of neoliberal policy topoi that emerged and then travelled globally at the end of the twentieth century, and I also investigate illustrations of these neoliberal policies' differing material and programmatic impact. These policies draw from common (and historically embedded) representations of the poor, attempt to change and make standard particular gendered ways of acting, and espouse neoliberal tenets of mainstreaming, fitness, and empowerment. By networking arguments, we can begin to effectively disentangle the commonplaces of public policy from their taken-for-granted meanings and show how they are not a single totalizing discourse but many interwoven strands of arguments. By untangling and exposing the contradictions in these arguments and considering their networked relationship to other policies, rhetoricians can demonstrate that policy can be a space of negotiation. For example, across the policies I examine in this book, colonial history still impacts how policy makers decide what Third World women need, and eugenicist ideologies influence how policy makers see poor women's needs. At the same time, my analysis shows the subtle differences in arguments, demonstrating how the material impact of topos is vastly different depending on context.

I organize my study around three transnational commonplaces—mainstreaming, fitness, and empowerment—and examine how the rise of neoliberal economics and enduring (neo)colonial ideologies at the end of the twentieth century are exigencies for particular policy arguments about women's place in the transnational economy. I focus on these terms specifically because all three emerge as seemingly common terms over and over again in gender policies at the end of the twentieth century and the beginning of the twenty-first century. Coming on the back of the United Nation's Decade for Women (1985–1995), this period also marks a time when women's issues came to the forefront not only of public policy but also in conversations about global development as a whole. I argue that to understand these policy and development arguments about women, rhetoricians must network arguments by considering the topoi, circulating logics, interarticulating arguments, and diverse contexts that link the domestic and international norms.

I aim to broaden rhetorical study so that rhetoricians might gauge the ways in which transnational movements have impacted our receptions of texts, generally, and public policy writing, specifically. Yet, in part due to neoliberal economics and neoliberal governmentality, I also seek to illustrate how rhetoricians must attend to the ways that the global policy writing depends upon the malleability of arguments; globalization does not have a single outcome but rather is an uneven movement that has brought both positive and negative changes across the globe (see McRuer). I show that even though the topoi of transnationalism might appear to be universal, they are not.

As each chapter will demonstrate further, each commonplace itself is noteworthy because the ways in which the term's meaning fluctuates within differing policy initiatives also demonstrates how pro-feminist and activist arguments are subtly co-opted, reassembled, and then reappropriated for vastly different uses. Yet, a careful rhetorical analysis must also look beyond reappropriation since there is not one common argument across each policy; rather, the individual policy's logic is situated in a broader network of transnational influences—history, actors, economies, and so on. Depending on the policy's context, gender mainstreaming arguments (for example) might draw on colonial discourses or racial and ethnic stereotypes thereby remarginalizing the very women the policy seeks to make "normal." Gender mainstreaming practices, therefore, cannot be deemed as inherently good or bad; rather, they illustrate how the cultural logics of transnationalism depend upon the malleability of terms so that, as these topoi travel across national boundaries, their meanings shift and change due to context, history, and even intention. In other words, these commonplaces are part of a network of transnational relationships that enable them to slip from and be repurposed for one context or another. Ultimately, *Networking Arguments* offers a rhetorical analysis of public policy but in doing so it also offers a different kind of rhetorical analysis that traces networks of distributed logics and shifting frames of reference, providing rhetoricians with an introduction to how transnational feminist theory can help us understand the rhetoricity of transnational public policies (or transnational texts in general).

2 GENDER MAINSTREAMING

Transnational rhetorics of gender mainstreaming are born out of the Fourth World Conference on Women held in Beijing, China (1995), and the conference's international guiding document the *Beijing Declaration and Platform for Action.*[1] At its basic definition, the *Beijing Declaration and Platform for Action* defines gender mainstreaming as the act of policy writers and makers considering the differing effects of policies on men and women respectively before putting those policies into action. Yet, as I began to discuss in chapter 1, the document as a whole importantly reveals how gender mainstreaming policies must *connect* women's local customs and circumstances to wider global, cultural, and economic shifts and the material results of supranational policies. In the Beijing Platform for Action, gender mainstreaming does not simply mean establishing policies that address gender disparities or examining how the policies will impact women and men differently. Rather, the Platform for Action suggests that effective gender mainstreaming practices must revise the development agenda at large so that each local agenda considers how it will impact women personally, socially, and economically *and* address specific issues that tend to pertain to women. Ultimately, the Beijing Platform claims that gender mainstreaming can only be achieved by introducing policy and development initiatives that address how gender disparities are caused by a complex matrix of situations that includes colonial history, postcolonial politics, supranational institutions (such as the International Monetary Fund or IMF, who promoted structural adjustment policies), local customs, and transnational power relationships (such as those manifested in trade agreements like NAFTA).

Governments, nongovernmental organizations (NGOs), and supranational institutions have taken the Beijing Platform recommendations quite seriously in part because it is an international guiding document endorsed by the United Nation's Development Fund for Women (UNIFEM) and by women across the globe. The Beijing conference, and the platform itself, set in motion other international meetings, new transnational organizations, and policy initiatives that sought to enact gender mainstreaming. For example, just back from Beijing, then first lady Hillary Clinton created the President's Interagency Council on Women in order to "make sure that all the effort and good ideas actually get implemented when we get back home" (Albright et al. 234), and, as I describe in chapter 1, in 1997 at its annual meeting, the World Bank made a formal commitment to gender equality through gender mainstreaming; since that time the Bank has implemented their Gender Action Plan, which promotes that "gender equality is smart economics" (Wolfensohn). Yet, overwhelmingly, the subsequent gender mainstreaming policies and development initiatives (such as these) that followed the Beijing Platform rhetorically construct gender mainstreaming to mean something quite different from the platform's recommendations.

Gender mainstreaming initiatives, which were conceived by feminists and women across the world as a way to deal with local and global structural inequalities, turned into policies that attempted to manage individual choices and intimate relationships. By tracing gender mainstreaming rhetorics from their inception at the Beijing conference through the World Bank, United Nations, and U.S. welfare policies and by following the term *gender mainstreaming* and its ideologies throughout diffuse documents, I show how post-Beijing gender mainstreaming arguments tend to assume that women are always (and only) vulnerable to local gender-based violence, do not see traditional women's work (such as care work or farming) as actual work, and do not recognize women as already deeply involved in their communities. As a result, the rhetoric of gender mainstreaming shifts from an argument about vectors of oppression to a patronizing and presumptive (colonialist and neoliberal) argument that positions the state or supranational organizations as the benevolent savior for women, without bothering to consider how women's needs or desires may vary based on their geopolitical location.

Yet, due to gender mainstreaming rhetorics' historic connection to a pro-woman conference and document (i.e., the Beijing Platform), within post-Beijing policies, gender mainstreaming as a term carries an unquestionable ethos that makes the policies that are organized around this term seem palpable, commonsense, and even feminist. Thus crucially, post-Beijing gender mainstreaming rhetorics draw from a variety of arguments and demonstrate the need for feminist rhetoricians to consider pretexts—before a text is actualized—when and how particular arguments are evoked, and what contextual networks give gender mainstreaming rhetorics clout. Even though gender mainstreaming might appear to be a transnationally and universally coherent term, when that term travels in policy networks, this rhetoric does not have "universal claims . . . [and thus does] not actually make everything everywhere the same" (Tsing 1) as the documents I explore suggest.

Rather, post Beijing, depending on the contexts in which policy makers employ the term *gender mainstreaming*, gender mainstreaming arguments have a tendency to mean a return to something familiar (dormant citizenship, family, safety, colonial order, or eugenic stereotypes, to name a few) without an analysis of the structural and networked conditions that so often impact gender inequalities. As Homi Bhabha has argued, colonial discourses persuade because they appear to be real, natural, and something that everybody knows and is familiar with; their repeatability sustains eugenic and colonial arguments and symbologies (both visual and textual). Thus, gender mainstreaming arguments allow audiences to identify with them precisely because, post Beijing, they maintain the static connotation of a presumed discourse that "we all know": that men, patriarchal cultures, and "backward" practices oppress women. In this way, gender mainstreaming rhetorics function as "common sense." These static connotations work against the networked gender mainstreaming arguments that the Bejing Platform promotes. In other words, audiences can easily identify with gender mainstreaming policies that appear to be organized around this presumption without considering the material or rhetorical work of the term *gender mainstreaming* within individual documents. As a result, policy makers easily pick up the topos of gender mainstreaming and repurpose it in a variety of contexts thereby actually making the term's meaning and material outcomes unclear and unstable.

My analysis shows that the rhetorical appeal of gender mainstreaming arguments appear common across policy spaces. Yet, as policy makers employ gender mainstreaming rhetorics, from policy to policy, they end up having no coherency or stability of meaning, making it necessary for rhetoricians to consider not only gender mainstreaming rhetorics as occasion bound but also how arguments for gender mainstreaming are affected by other powerful contexts such as geopolitical economic relations, colonial consciousnesses, and gendered labor conditions.

The way policy makers and development experts translate the term *gender mainstreaming* into policy documents should be a crucial concern for feminist rhetoricians because this act of translation demonstrates how arguments shift and change due to economic and geopolitical contexts and thus shows how power informs rhetorics. For this reason, I situate the rhetoric of gender mainstreaming within the rise of neoliberal economics and enduring neocolonialism—both forms of power—at the end of the twentieth century in order to identify the exigencies for and varying rhetorical appeals of these policies. In doing so, I also offer the term *transcoding* as a new rhetorical concept that can help rhetoricians identify how policy writers resituate a taken-for-granted term like *gender mainstreaming* to fit with varying policy agendas.

While the term *transcoding* describes the practice of translating digital data so that it works in several platforms, Inderpal Grewal has adopted the term *transcode* to describe how neoliberal logics (and I would add, rhetorics) travel along transnational networks, subtly shifting and changing to fit various situations while seemingly maintaining a common ideology (23). Following Grewal's reification of the term and its original meaning, to change data while keeping to the data's integrity, I use rhetorical transcoding to mean "the process of directly changing assembled code to work on different platforms" ("Transcoding"). Transcoding thus aptly describes how gender mainstreaming rhetorics function in policy texts; on one level the meaning of gender mainstreaming is unquestioned, on the other it rhetorically functions to mean something slightly different depending on context, occasion, and audience.

Rhetorical transcoding draws attention to the fact that as rhetorics move they do not always carry the same ideological assumptions. Rhetorical meaning is not always directly translated across documents, and as rhetorics move, their meanings may shift to fit with various political agendas such as the implementation of neoliberal economics across the globe. Activists from around the world (many of whom identified as feminists) first put forth gender mainstreaming rhetorics, but policy makers (working for nation-states and supranational institutions) reinterpret, transcode, and implement these rhetorics.

Rhetorics move then from the scale of conference and guiding document to the scale of nation-state or supranation-state. The Beijing Platform responded, presumably, to women's situated knowledge and was written by women (and men) who had these women's best interests in mind. However, as the document travels from Beijing to states and supranational institutions, which have different interests than the people who work directly with populations, the states and institutions that implement gender mainstreaming policies are interested in producing coherent and manageable populations and therefore employ commonsense ideas about women and gender that are often in conflict with the Beijing Platform. Without examining how rhetorics move, feminist rhetoricians would not see the diverse rhetorical and material work of arguments for gender mainstreaming.

As I described in chapter 1, feminist studies of rhetoric have predominantly focused more on occasion-bound, historical recovery work and in doing so have identified marginalized voices, specifically uncovering the unique ways women and racial and ethnic minorities move audiences to action. While these studies have explored the relationship between language and power, they have not examined the *pretexts* of recovery work. Before marginalized voices can be recovered, before audiences can be moved to action, we need to understand networked power and how the process of moving texts from one scale to another can have the effect of *further* silencing women. Paying attention to rhetorical transcoding brings awareness to the wider contexts that enable some discourse on and about women to circulate and others not. In addition, tracing rhetorical transcoding can help feminist rhetoricians identify how power operates in transnational networks affecting women's material realities and sometimes constraining their voices. As a tangible example of how this power works on a rhetorical and then material level, we might think about how in the United States colonial ideologies about Muslim women's (lack of) agency served as a pretext for U.S. policies and aid to Afghanistan post–9/11; much of the aid and development initiatives from the United States focused on veiling, an issue many Muslim women from the region did not see as a problem (see Hesford and Kozol). Most women from Afghanistan were more concerned about poverty, widowhood, their children's health, and their ability to make money. As this grounded example makes clear, pretexts have material effects. As such, my rhetorical analysis in this chapter then also offers feminist recovery efforts a rich and specific examination of power as it works in various contexts by linking recovery to neocolonial discourses and neoliberal economics. In other words, before we examine women's rhetorical acts, it is useful to look at how policy documents stand for and represent women.

The gender mainstreaming policies I examine are diverse; they range from an international guiding document to a national policy to a supranational development plan. Looking at these documents together shows how arguments are transcoded to fit within a neocolonial and neoliberal market logic, thus demonstrating how ideologies and global changes enable international gendered logics to become national and international norms (and vice versa) and showing the importance of tracing rhetorics across time and texts.

By tracing how policy makers transcode rhetorics, I illustrate that rhetorics are not static and that transcoding has material effects on women. In some instances, for example, post-Beijing neoliberal gender mainstreaming policies triple the hours of women's workdays, making them responsible for family care, formal labor, and food production and thereby affecting women's mental and physical health. In other cases, gender mainstreaming policies construct women as not attached to their families and other times as overly attached to their families and in doing so legislate that women must be more active at home or less active respectively. Although, at the level of discourse, gender mainstreaming rhetorics may look static, by paying attention to the arguments and contexts that surround (and network to) those rhetorics, rhetoricians can trace the subtle shifts in signification as rhetorics travel and in doing so reveal how networked power and contexts impact the representation of women. The original intention of gender mainstreaming, for example, was to "transform organizations" and policy initiatives so that they materially reflect a culture of diversity by making it possible for people with a variety of backgrounds and from various geopolitical locales to have their needs and desires met in an increasingly global economy (Bacchi and Eveline 101). Yet, since the Beijing conference, policies transcode the rhetoric of gender mainstreaming to support the transnational neoliberal goals of expanding global capitalism, lessening government-led social services, and implementing rational choice economics;[2] these policies have predominately had a negative impact on women. In other words, gender mainstreaming rhetorics become malleable and policy makers carefully craft them to fit neoliberal policy agendas. To meet these neoliberal goals, gender mainstreaming policies may *appear to* support a culture of diversity, so to speak; however, the policies work to make standard and coherent familial arrangements, work, ontologies, and economic practices.

Post-Beijing neoliberal gender mainstreaming policies attempt to change women so that they fit into a global capitalist equation rather than considering how to address differences, inequalities, and poverty in a socially and contextually appropriate way. Neoliberal gender mainstreaming arguments craft individual citizens from low-income nations as transformed workers who can facilitate market and global labor activities that not only enable their nation to be a part of the transnational economy but also be solely responsible for their own economic well-being. These policies represent women as workers who, through their own determination to change their ways of being, can secure their financial resources rather than working to change the relations of power that marginalize them in the first place.

The World Bank and the United States' policy logic, for instance, is that women will keep to the policy's demands if it means their families will be economically (and thus physically) secured. It follows from this argument then that the state does not need to use its resources to support citizens because they have become economically independent. To concentrate on women, with their presumed "natural" instinct to protect their families, appears to make good "policy sense." And yet, although gender mainstreaming policies purport to be in the best interest of women, some nations' gender mainstreaming policies have resulted in a reduction of women-centered policy initiatives. In addition, post-Beijing gender mainstreaming policies follow the neoliberal argument (and then to this extent become part of the discourse of neoliberalism) that governments should only manage social services from afar and not get directly involved with those services; however, these policies allocate social services to the market, going against the Beijing Platform's recommendation that *governments* (*Beijing Declaration* 5), not the private sector, work to mainstream a gender perspective into all levels of policy. As Carol Bacchi and Joan

Eveline describe, gender mainstreaming policy logics often construct women's gendered activities as an enterprise that global businesses might "tap into" and profit from (105). By networking gender mainstreaming arguments to the context of neoliberalism, policy makers transcode gender mainstreaming rhetorics so that policies do not deal with structural inequalities as the Beijing Platform intended but rather they reinforce the very gendered structures that make gender mainstreaming necessary in the first place. Gender mainstreaming policy arguments ultimately tend to focus on individual achievement and not structural change.

NETWORKING GENDER MAINSTREAMING ARGUMENTS

The Beijing Platform for Action demonstrates the difficulty of analyzing the rhetoric of public policy because there is quite literally no one specific author or writer; UN delegates brought a draft (with about one-third of it bracketed for discussion and revision) to the Beijing conference and then that draft was revised based on conference participants' statements and negotiations. Because the Beijing Platform is an international guiding document, meaning that the policy seeks to guide governments and organizations for best practices in promoting women's equality, analyzing just the platform does not fully address the material effects of gender mainstreaming rhetorics. Yet, to understand how gender mainstreaming rhetorics become transcoded in various documents, one must first understand the Beijing Platform and its occasion-bound rhetorics of gender mainstreaming. Studying the rhetoric of gender mainstreaming in the Beijing Platform reveals how the document attempts to reflect a variety of women's needs from across the world and shows how the document networks and connects context-based arguments to create a holistic definition of gender mainstreaming.

There are few studies of how the Beijing Platform for Action actually came together. While scholars and journalists note that the concept of gender mainstreaming was first spoken about in 1985 at the Third Conference on Women in Nairobi, Kenya, it was not until the Beijing Fourth World Conference that participants drafted an official policy for gender mainstreaming. As mentioned earlier, the Beijing Platform reflects discussions originating in Nairobi and from a series of speeches that national government and international organization representatives presented at the beginning of the conference. These representatives spent much of the remaining Beijing conference arguing over the language of the Platform for Action and how to best represent the diverse and sometime conflicting needs and voices of women. There are moments in the Beijing Platform where we can see how participants and writers sought to best represent women's diversity; for example, the Beijing Platform states that "it respects and values the full diversity of women's situations and conditions and recognizes that some women face particular barriers to their empowerment" (7) and then goes on to note them: "race, age, language, ethnicity, culture, religion, or disability" (4). However, snippets of disagreements appear in newspaper articles and NGO reports from people attending the conference, but there are no physical traces of the conversations that actually formed the final Platform for Action. This is a conundrum for rhetoricians because they must piece together conversations (sometimes translated from a variety of languages or through the lens of a reporter) from these reports to get a sense of the rhetorical work of the Beijing Platform.

For example, the *Washington Times* describes the conflict between groups of mostly secular women who supported women's right to abortion versus non-secular women from across religious sects who felt that the conference had been "hijacked . . . and that some delegates were promoting adultery . . . free sex" and "boys and girls being allowed to have sex without being married" ("World's Women Convene"). This article likewise reports disagreements in how the Beijing Platform represented the traditional family. While the now late Prime Minister Benazir Bhutto (Pakistan), for instance, stated that the first draft of the Beijing Platform was "notably weak on the role of the traditional family," Donna Shalala (U.S.A) countered by observing that "our reading of the document is that it is very much a mild document and in support of the family" ("World's Women Convene"). Other media outlets describe how Beijing participants fought over the use of the term *gender*, citing that some participants claimed that it referred to sexuality or sexual practices and while others defined it as culturally derived roles for males and females ("War Over Words Divides UN Women's Conference"). These examples demonstrate that there were myriad actors who aided in writing and revising the Beijing Platform and that the final draft did attempt to include the needs and sometimes conflicting desires of women from lower-income nations, religious and secular organizations, and governments.

Given that there were so many actors contributing language and arguments to the Beijing Platform, rhetoricians might read the document as a policy that reflects the unity of women—the notion that women across the world worked together to reach consensus. However, the lens of transnational feminism is attentive to how language, culture, geopolitical location, history, and international and supranational power relationships affect arguments and representations and thus emphasizes difference and incongruity over unity. As a result, I interpret the language of the Beijing Platform as both a compromise (and not necessarily a unified compromise) between these conflicting voices and as a document that honors differences. Because the Beijing Platform was essentially written by a diverse set of people and that diverse set of people tended to come from a privileged class (i.e., they all came from a class who could travel to and stay in Beijing) the document cannot be read as reflecting *all* women's needs per se; rather it must be read as a negotiated document that attempts to reflect needs that may be in conflict. Thus, to perform a transnational feminist rhetorical analysis means highlighting how this compromise appears in the nuanced rhetoric of gender mainstreaming that networks the wider contexts that impact women's diverse experiences.

For example, the Beijing Platform showcases traces of human rights discourses as well as what we might identify as neoliberal discourses—two discourses that are often in conflict with each other. Wendy Brown notes that human rights discourses (relying upon liberal democracy and liberal humanism) tend to privilege doing what is morally right versus neoliberal discourses that tend to promote practices that weigh the financial costs and benefits of a policy or practice over the good of the people (Brown, "Neo-libralism"; *Regulating Aversion*). However, what is interesting is that in the Beijing Platform these discourses work together and, in doing so, gesture to moments of negotiation between conference participants. For instance, even though the Beijing Platform partially defines gender mainstreaming as women having the ability to work outside the home and earn an income, it also says that women have the *right* to earn a living wage and the *right* to have access to needed social and health services (12, 10). Likewise, the Beijing Platform locates part of women's oppression both in their ever-expanding workday (i.e., domestic, formal, and farming and sustaining labor) and in gendered expectations (12). The post-Beijing documents, however, tend to define gender mainstreaming as only preparing women (or quite literally changing women's behaviors) to be "independent" so that they can work outside the home (i.e., participate in the formal market and in neoliberal economy). Following transnational feminist theory, then, I do not read the Beijing Platform's rhetoric of gender mainstreaming as good or bad, but rather I read the document for how both neoliberal and human rights arguments network with each other and with wider contexts in importantly productive ways. To this extent, the Beijing Platform indirectly addresses Brown's concerns about the material results of liberal and neoliberal ideologies.

The ways in which the Beijing Platform melds human rights discourses and neoliberal discourses can be seen in the following example. The Beijing Platform states that it seeks to "promote women's economic independence, including employment, and eradicate the persistent and increasing burden of poverty on women by addressing the structural causes of poverty through changes in economic structures, ensuring equal access for all women, including those in rural areas, as vital development agents, to productive resources, opportunities and public services" (4). While this statement begins by noting the importance of supporting women's economic independence—part of the core values of neoliberalism—it counters this neoliberal aim by connecting women's poverty to structural roots and not to women's own tenacity (also part of the neoliberal discourse I explore in post-Beijing documents and in subsequent chapters). In addition, this statement specifically connects the notion that women's economic independence depends upon changes to larger economic arrangements *and* access to public services. Following a moral argument, it notes that women have become overly burdened by poverty due to issues beyond their control: structural causes such as war, postcolonial governments, and changes to the global economy to name a few. In this example, women's economic independence is networked to the need for governments and supranational agencies to change wider structures of poverty, including making sure women have access to necessary public services; thus economic independence becomes part of the rhetoric of gender mainstreaming only insofar as this independence is supported by larger economic structures. Not working wholly with or against neoliberalism or liberal humanism, this statement reveals gender mainstreaming arguments that rhetorically connect development initiatives, gender equity, public services, and economic changes. Annex 1, which precedes the official Platform for Action, similarly demonstrates the idea of networking gender mainstreaming initiatives to wider contexts. It notes that across the globe, women's inequality is "exacerbated by the increasing poverty that is affecting the lives of the majority of the world's people, in particular women and children," and this increase has "origins in both the national and international domains" (*Beijing Declaration* 1). The foreword's claims are further unpacked in the larger Beijing Platform where successful gender mainstreaming approaches are attached to revising larger supranational development projects. The Beijing Platform, for example, peripatetically explains how poorly designed structural adjustment policies, unequal education programs, excessive military expenditures (over social programs), and disproportionate global economic growth has distinct material effects and has led to the feminization of poverty and has specifically affected women in low-income nations, not only economically but also socially and culturally (10). Widespread and global economic recessions lead to political and social unrest and, as a result, unduly influence women's well-being; these global changes have led governments to seek loans and development aid from organizations such as the IMF and World Bank and from wealthier nations. However, this aid and these loans have often forced countries to impose structural adjustment programs, which inflate the cost of local products that are not imported while at the same time devaluing local currencies and making both local and imported necessities immensely expensive.[3]

The Beijing Platform for Action networks women's poverty to the need for gender mainstreaming policies that address the wrath of structural adjustment polices: "structural adjustment programmes have not been designed to minimize their negative effects on vulnerable and disadvantaged groups or on women, nor have they been designed to assure positive effects on those groups by preventing their marginalization in economic and social activities" (*Beijing Declaration* 10). In this example, women's disenfranchisement is not connected to deep-seated (or assumed "backward") cultural practices or individual choices (as my analysis of post-Beijing documents below will suggest), but rather it is *caused* by the poor design of these development programs as well as "increased unemployment and underemployment" (10). This overt critique of structural adjustment policies coupled with the Beijing Platform's use of the words *disadvantaged*, *vulnerable*, and *marginalized* demonstrates how the writers of the document were very much working against the free market and neoliberal ideologies, which many IMF and World Bank development programs tend to support, by recognizing the importance and legitimacy of the state sustaining programs such as health care and welfare—programs that in many nations were born out the goals of liberal humanism (and sometimes, especially during the era of decolonization, alongside pressure from state socialisms that provided a more egalitarian competing model of public services). This, coupled with the fact that earlier the Beijing Platform notes that "it respects and values the full diversity of women's situations and conditions and recognizes that some women face particular barriers to their empowerment" (7), shows how the Beijing Platform has a nuanced understanding of the vectors of oppressions, the local and global causes, and structural dynamics that may impact women's well-being and ability to participate in their communities.

While according to many post-Beijing policies, development that is attentive to gender mainstreaming means that low-income countries must lower their trade barriers, grow their economies, and enter global capitalism, the Beijing Platform notes the limitations of this plan specifically for women. The Beijing Platform references decisions taking place at the Uruguay Round of Multilateral Trade (1994) and notes how due to "the increasing interdependence of national economies, as well as the importance of trade liberalization and access to open, dynamic markets," there has been a remarkable decline in official development assistance reaching vulnerable populations (*Beijing Declaration* 10). This connection between unequal trade policies among nations and women's poverty demonstrates that global economic partnerships often are not in the best interest of women. In fact, as the Beijing Platform makes clear, such policies must integrate a nuanced gender mainstreaming perspective and examine how trade agreements might impact women and men differently, especially as women tend to bear the brunt of poverty for their families and communities. The Beijing Platform also notes that in some cases policies between nations can support extreme gender discrimination because they exacerbate postcolonial and neocolonial power relationships where women end up shouldering newly established governments and "customary" cultural practices that further marginalize them in the name of tradition. As these examples illustrate, the Beijing Platform connects women's poverty to a diverse set of contexts that might at first appear to indirectly impact women.

The Beijing Platform then networks gender mainstreaming to less obvious material effects, specifically suggesting that the process of gender mainstreaming can improve women's local and global communities. The document, for example, notes that "local, national, regional and global peace is . . . inextricably linked with the advancement of women, who are a fundamental force for leadership, conflict resolution and the promotion of lasting peace at all levels" (*Beijing Declaration* 3). While this statement might be read as a blind celebration of women as peacemakers or as assuming that all women are (or can be) peacemakers, the Beijing Platform goes on to show how gender mainstreaming is part of the cornerstone for local, regional, and global peace and in doing so networks the positive results of gender mainstreaming to material and visceral issues such as war and ethnic conflict. In doing so, the Beijing Platform asks nations and organizations to: "take positive steps to ensure peace for the advancement of women and, recognizing the leading role that women have played in the peace movement, work actively towards general and complete disarmament under strict and effective international control, and support negotiations on the conclusion, without delay, of a universal and multilaterally and effectively verifiable comprehensive nuclear-test-ban treaty which contributes to nuclear disarmament and the prevention of the proliferation of nuclear weapons in all its aspects" (4). This statement integrates neoliberal and human rights discourses by focusing on individual women's role in global peace but also notes the role of the state, other organizations, and nations in supporting disarmament. Yet, additionally, the statement networks together women's involvement in local and global peace movements with resisting poverty, noting that when women are not in poverty they are more likely to be able to work to secure peace not only in their own communities but also in the global community. War is not only a women's issue because women need to be involved in disarmament; war is also a disruptive technology that has gendered effects. Later, the Beijing Platform notes how heavy military spending by governments in some regions of the world has come at the expense of social development, health, and other in-kind programs; these sorts of programs indirectly aid in advancing women (10). As the Beijing Platform clearly states: "the social dimension of development should be emphasized" (4) over a focus on an individual woman's (or country's) development. Keeping women out of poverty, ensuring their access to health programs, and tapping into already established women's antiwar connections could ultimately result in global peace.

As the above example shows, not only do the writers of the Beijing Platform balance a variety of political agendas, they also network global security to women's involvement in peace movements, to their material conditions (such as keeping their family and community out of poverty), and to the fact that to be involved they must have physical welfare. However, women's well-being (as well as men's) is not possible unless there are larger global and local structures in place that allow women to make an adequate income, have health care, child care, and a safe home. The Beijing Platform also connects individual women's and community security to a safe and healthy environment: "We are deeply convinced that economic development, social development and environmental protection are interdependent and mutually reinforcing components of sustainable development, which is the framework for our efforts to achieve a higher quality of life for all people. Equitable social development that recognizes empowering the poor, particularly women living in poverty, to utilize environmental resources sustainably is a necessary foundation for sustainable development. We also recognize that broad-based and sustained economic growth in the context of sustainable development is necessary to sustain social development and social justice" (*Beijing Declaration* 5). This example plainly illustrates that women's well-being is even connected with sustainable development. Without having access to unpolluted environmental resources, women will not be able to flourish. As the Beijing Platform makes undoubtedly clear, a gender mainstreaming perspective on development must connect women's (and men's) needs to every aspect of their lives:

> Absolute poverty and the feminization of poverty, unemployment, the increasing fragility of the environment, continued violence against women and the widespread exclusion of half of humanity from institutions of power and governance underscore the need to continue the search for development, peace and security and for ways of assuring people-centered sustainable development. The participation and leadership of the half of humanity that is female is essential to the success of that search. Therefore, only a new era of international cooperation among Governments and peoples based on a spirit of partnership, an equitable, international social and economic environment, and a radical transformation of the relationship between women and men to one of full and equal partnership will enable the world to meet the challenges of the twenty-first century. (10)

To address these issues, the Beijing Platform suggests that women themselves make decisions regarding development and in turn influence the development priorities and activities put forth by supranational and local governments. These examples make it clear that gender mainstreaming, according to the Beijing Platform, means developing policies, programs, and practices that do not simply respond to gender inequality but that actually encourage cultural practices that positively impact women and their diverse needs.

In the Beijing Platform, gender mainstreaming means addressing the ways in which women's equality relates to women's rights as human rights as well attending to national and global infrastructures so that women, aided by their government, develop the (personal) ability to resist impoverishment, participate in public and private decision making, work outside the home (if individual women choose to do so), and influence media representations of women and girls. Yet, the rhetorical and material work of the Beijing Platform and gender mainstreaming policies at large cannot be understood unless we look beyond the formal production of such a policy and its localized arguments. Instead, to understand the impact of the Beijing Platform, rhetoricians must consider how subsequent policies transcode the term *gender mainstreaming*—discursively, historically, and contextually. Certainly, as Bacchi and Eveline note: "Policies do not simply 'impact' on people; they 'create' people" (110). Thus we need to consider how policies discursively create particular classes of people, reproduce dominant power relationships, and reinforce gendered, raced, and geopolitical expectations through their transcoding of gender mainstreaming.

TRANSCODING GENDER MAINSTREAMING

Following the Fourth World Conference on Women, between 1996 and 1997, the World Bank and the United States both enrolled antipoverty policies and programs that integrated a gender mainstreaming perspective. However, unlike the Beijing Platform, these policies tended to center on women as core economic actors and also how to *change* women so that they might fit into the evolving neoliberal economy. As I began to describe in chapter 1, Brown (following Foucault) identifies neoliberalism as a sort of governmentality, "a mode of governance encompassing but not limited to the state, one that produces subjects, forms of citizenship and behavior" ("Neo-liberalism"). In other words, Brown makes clear that neoliberalism is not only a political or economic philosophy but rather it imbues our ways of being and acting in subtle ways. Both the World Bank and the United States transcoded the meaning of gender mainstreaming in notable ways—ways that at once work with and contradict each other and the Beijing Platform. Policy makers transcode gender mainstreaming rhetorics into a neoliberal discourse that means changing individual behaviors, family structures, and ontologies while at the same time reducing social services—all things that work directly against the networked gender mainstreaming arguments that are present in the Beijing Platform. In these examples, policy makers center on individual women's economic security and familial relationships, assuming that across cultures women generally place their families' well-being above their own. The World Bank and the United States transcode gender mainstreaming into a policy logic that presumes that women will keep to the policy if it means their families will be economically (and thus physically) secured. Following neoliberal economics, then, this arrangement would shirk state power while bolstering the private sector so that the state would be able to use fewer of its resources to support its citizens. To concentrate on individual women's behaviors, their supposed "natural" instinct to protect their families, and their unpaid labor in the home appears to be an extremely neoliberal version of gender mainstreaming—a version that demonstrates what Brown calls neoliberal governmentality. The neoliberal logic that women must be changed, and the logic that cultural patriarchy gets in the way of the new global economy, demonstrates how a transcoded rhetoric of gender mainstreaming folds into neoliberal and neocolonial discourses.

Despite the Beijing Platform's very clear definition of gender mainstreaming and nuanced understanding of the need to address issues of gender inequality in regards to social programs, development practices, and neocolonial power relations, and despite global policy makers' vocal and public support for gender mainstreaming initiatives, welfare programs across the world began to falter post Beijing, resulting in uneven policies that have adversely affected women by widening the economic disparity between men and women. In part due to the IMF structural adjustment and currency devaluation policies and World Bank economic development programs, post Beijing many poor nations across the globe ultimately had to reduce the very social programs designed to help women succeed in the paid labor market (Rittich 249). In addition to devaluing many nations' currencies, structural adjustment policies also asked nations to cut maternity, disability, sickness safety nets, and education programs and constrict access to family cash allowances, in-kind benefits, and other state-supported social programs such as education. These happenings reflect state restructuring of social benefits (reduction of the role of the welfare state) across the globe. These changes both made more necessary and yet limited the gender mainstreaming initiatives conceived in Beijing. Despite strong support for gender mainstreaming from the global community, the subsequent gender mainstreaming policies and programs in no way reflected the Beijing Platform. Because the platform had been transcoded, although wealthier nations voiced support for gender mainstreaming initiatives, similar social policy changes also took place in the United States and throughout Europe just as many nations entered the European Union. Such changes, for example, can be found in the infamous Personal Responsibility and Work Opportunity Reconciliation Act of 1996 (the welfare bill to "end welfare as we know it") and the congressional debates that surrounded it.

The U.S. welfare debates occurred on the heels of the Beijing conference for women and just after both former President and First Lady Clinton formally supported gender mainstreaming initiatives at home through their creation of the President's Interagency Council on Women. Yet despite the U.S. government's celebration of the Beijing conference, within the U.S. Personal Responsibility Act and the debates that surround it, gender mainstreaming becomes transcoded by focusing on women's and men's gender role behaviors. For example, in the congressional hearing Reinventing Welfare, which preceded the Personal Responsibility Act's enrollment, Judith M. Gueron suggested welfare policies must "change whom [the policy] serve[s], not how [the policy] serve[s] people" (qtd. in Deprez 37). Gueron's statement follows the same neoliberal logic espoused by the World Bank gender mainstreaming policies that I began to discuss in chapter 1: that it is culture, ontology, and behavior, not politics or the economy, that determine the success of a nation. As I discussed previously, in Wolfensohn's 1997 annual address he not only suggests that the World Bank must make the "unfit fit," but he also adds that it is necessary to bring women "into the mainstream of the economy." To make this plan appear viable, the World Bank employs archetypical colonial symbologies of women that render them "underdeveloped" and thus in need of being saved by the capitalist economy. Because the Bank depicts women as powerless and sometimes even "primitive," they illustrate that investors and development experts need to create policy interventions that would make women viable entrepreneurs. The United States' welfare policy similarly portrays welfare-using women as "backward": amoral and unmarried and physically, mentally, and cognitively harming their children. The U.S. Personal Responsibility Act argues that to prepare women for the neoliberal economy the policy must attempt to make women better caregivers inside and workers outside the home through the institution of marriage. The examples below demonstrate how the rhetoric of gender mainstreaming is transcoded from the Beijing Platform—where gender mainstreaming means connecting women's well-being to wider contextual factors such as the global economy, local infrastructures, and colonial history—before thinking about how individuals might act. Instead policy makers argue that to make welfare recipients and Third World women viable economic actors they must be fundamentally changed.

In 1997, for example, just two years after the Beijing conference and very much in response to the Beijing Platform's gender mainstreaming initiative, the World Bank publicly announced that women are the keys to a nation's economic success (and as I discuss in chapter 3, in 2004, the World Bank follows in a similar vein to announce people with disabilities as the key to successful national development). In a speech called "The Challenge of Inclusion," given by then Bank president James Wolfensohn, he stated that it was time for the World Bank to make a formal commitment specifically to include women in global development. He begins the speech in this way:

> I have learned that people are the same wherever they are—here in this room and across the world. We all want the best for our children and our families. We all want peace and economic and physical security. We all want to live in a supportive community. We all want personal dignity.
>
> This was vividly brought home to me six months ago when I visited a large water and sanitation project. . . . [I] went from one makeshift home to the next, talking with the women who live there and who used to carry water on their shoulders from the bottom of the hillside to their dwelling at the top. . . . And as I walked around, more and more of the women came up to me displaying pieces of paper showing charges and receipts for a few reals a month. I watched and listened to this until the vice governor said, "What they are showing you Jim, is that this is the first time in their lives that their name and address have appeared on an official notice. This is the first time their existence has been officially recognized. This is the first time they have been included in society." (1–2)

This story demonstrates the Bank's concentration on extending partnerships with women as "agents of development." Although, as I discuss further in chapter 4, in the past the Bank had given attention to women via programs such as Women in Development (WID), up until this point, the WID had been a marginalized part of the World Bank, and women's and gender issues under the WID tended to be tied to development concerns such as population control (Bergeron, *Fragments* 405).[4] As Suzanne Bergeron notes, before Wolfensohn's presidency, gender and other issues of inclusion were not part of the Bank's general protocol (Bergeron, "Challenging the World Bank"). Thus, Wolfensohn's speech, which contains an emotionally laden story whereby women are given entry into the market and therefore access to the global economy through their purchasing power, is a direct result of the Beijing conference and one of the first specific examples of how the World Bank began to transcode gender mainstreaming away from the Beijing Platform's holistic definition.

While Wolfensohn's focus on the "inclusion" of women (and other marginalized groups) does demonstrate the Bank's recognition that women may have different development needs than men, to resolve "The Challenge of Inclusion," Wolfensohn employs a rhetoric of gender mainstreaming that ultimately connects poverty alleviation for women to neoliberal market activities without noting the structural, cultural, or economic contexts that may limit women's ability to participate in such activities. Moreover, the classed system of capitalism, including transnational policy agreements and structural adjustment programs, which the Beijing Platform suggests greatly impacts women's inequality, becomes part of Wolfensohn's (and then the World Bank's) rhetoric of gender mainstreaming; the speech implies that the water system is *owned* by another entity. Wolfensohn's lengthy personal anecdote of visiting with poor women from the slums of some unnamed city in Brazil, intended to demonstrate the power and compassion of the World Bank, concludes with a group of women finally being "mainstreamed" through a receipt for a necessity like water. In this speech, Wolfensohn reframes the Beijing notion of gender mainstreaming to simply mean recognizing women and then putting their name on a receipt, which shows that the women paid money for a necessity like water. According to Wolfensohn's narrative, in which he rhetorically transcodes the Beijing concept of gender mainstreaming, it is the receipt with the women's names written on it, which signifies the women's entry into the market, that gives these women an identity. In other words, through this process of writing (i.e., having their name written on a receipt) as recognition, women merely become "mainstreamed" into the formal economy; he does not put forth context-based gender mainstreaming initiatives.

Going against the Beijing definition of gender mainstreaming, which means honoring women's differences and considering how their needs relate to wider and interconnected contexts, according to Wolfensohn, an ordinary receipt with the women's names written on it brings the poor Brazilian women into a recognizable historic trajectory and symbolizes the creation of an infrastructure—order, law, institutions, economic practices, and customs—as though these were not present before. In the Hegelian sense, writing is a form of gender mainstreaming and not only offers evidence of existence and history but it also indicates that there is "the possibility of history in a teleological sense" (Spurr 98). This writing implies the entrance into a language and economic practice that has meaning for people beyond local borders; writing means modernity. To this extent, the receipt for water service these women receive is, for Wolfensohn, the first step in creating a chronicled global presence—it is a physical reference of gender mainstreaming. Gender mainstreaming according to this speech becomes part of a neoliberal discourse that means putting women on a path toward formal market activities without recognizing the wide-reaching vectors of oppression and exploitation that impoverish women.

Wolfensohn used this speech to argue that it was time for the World Bank and development experts to mainstream gender and women's places in the development process; it was time, he concluded, to "include" women and bring "into society [those people] who have never been part of it before." Later in the speech, Wolfensohn went on to define the "challenge of inclusion" as "bringing more people into the economic mainstream" in order to "make the unfit fit." However, "making the unfit fit" also becomes making familial structures coherent and "normal."

In the beginning of the above story, Wolfensohn successfully consubstantiates his audience by asking them to imagine that their deepest concerns—those about their family, their physical and economic well-being—are the same as anybody else's. In doing so, Wolfenshon further transcodes gender mainstreaming to mean making the women of Brazil "normal." These women have been brought into recognizable citizenship through the process of economic "empowerment" and normalcy. In this example, normalcy functions through the World Bank providing women a history, what Francis Fukuyama recognizes as the end of history—when we have all been incorporated into the capitalist economy —and therefore implies that gender mainstreaming means the erasure of difference, not only physical, racial, or economic difference but also the difference produced by location, mind-set, desires, circumstance, and so on. As my analysis of the Beijing Platform makes clear, gender mainstreaming initiatives are meant to respect and work with women's diverse needs, experiences, and desires.

If indeed, in the words of Wolfensohn, "people are the same," then he also implies that people who fall outside the realms of "development" will not have the capability to fit in with the rest of the "developed" world *unless* they become part of the global market; this transcodes gender mainstreaming so that it fits into a neoliberal market logic whereby women must become like those women in the so-called developed world. Such a blind (and self-interested) celebration of women's independence without the recognition of local and global power structures, for example, which the Beijing Platform suggests greatly impacts women's inequality, becomes the great equalizer that erases gender and geopolitical, racial, and physical differences. Wolfensohn's appeal to individualism—part of the evolving neoliberal discourse of the time— reminds the audience of the Bank's larger project to make citizens individual actors who can secure their own economic viability by becoming similar to, or the same as, "successfully" developed countries.

Wolfensohn's transcoding of gender mainstreaming quite clearly demonstrates what Brown identifies as neoliberal governmentality. Although he connects gender mainstreaming to market activities, Wolfensohn also illustrates how neoliberal policy and development initiatives reach the "soul of the citizen-subject" by "*extending and disseminating market values to all institutions and social action*" (Brown, "Neo-libralism"), including intimate spaces like the family and the regulation of sexuality. Through a rhetoric of gender mainstreaming, Wolfensohn also portrays the women of the Brazilian favelas in classic colonial imagery thereby showing that these women need to be taught how to be proper global citizens. While Brown discusses govermentality in relationship to the nation-state, Wolfensohn's transcoding of gender mainstreaming demonstrates global governmentality through a supranational organization's project to make women into coherent citizens.

In this way, Wolfensohn's story depends upon his audience's identification of colonial texts. This story, where a group of formerly excluded women become active citizens of the globe, evokes the common representation of the colonized woman as either dangerous or a passive victim (Briggs 191). Wolfensohn's description of his experience in the Brazilian favelas is reminiscent of colonial narratives that describe non-Western countries as lacking, without history, devoid of a place or presence. His speech implies that the audience, made up of World Bank affiliates, is working to fill a void, making an impact, and creating an identity for a place that, before the Bank's intervention, was nameless or unviable—without an identity. This depiction makes the extension of neoliberal practices seem necessary—for they will make the women's lives legitimate (Brown, "Neo-liberalism"). Whereas the Beijing Platform recognizes that in successful gender mainstreaming initiatives women must be at the forefront of their own development projects (*Beijing Declaration* 3), Wolfensohn transcodes gender mainstreaming to reflect power relationships so development initiatives come from above and women themselves have little agency.

David Spurr calls this rhetorical trope negation: a discourse that "denies history as well as place, constituting the past as absence, but also designating that absence as a negative presence" (98). Although Spurr is speaking of the embedded and reified colonial and contemporary narratives about the African continent, his observations shed light on the binary logic that the whole of Wolfensohn's speech employs. The receipt with the women's names that Wolfensohn mentions is a physical marker of existence. At the end of his story he claims, "this is what the challenge of development is all about—inclusion. Bringing people into society who have never been part of it before. This is why the World Bank Group exists" (2). Ultimately, in this simple speech, Wolfensohn transcodes gender mainstreaming to reflect global governmentality, meaning that inclusion in the global capitalist economy erases the needs of women.

I want to note that, of course, the Brazilian women Wolfensohn describes may be experiencing the material realities of their country's developing market economy—the localized availability of clean drinking and cooking water and sanitary toilet and bathing facilities cuts down on time the women must spend fetching and preparing necessities like water. In this way, they are part of the larger story that is told about globalization and are an identifiable example of "success" in the global economy. However, as Bacchi and Eveline note: "So long as the focus remains on presumed biological characteristics, a neoliberal argument for freeing up economic arrangements to encourage individual success is uncontested. By contrast, insisting that 'difference' emerges from relationships of power rather than inhering in individuals or members of particular groups puts those relationships and the factors sustaining them under critical scrutiny" (109). Wolfensohn's argument for gender mainstreaming merely connects gender to biology, and in doing so he does not network to other contexts that may have disenfranchised the women from the favelas—instead, the women become a metonym for all other women. In this transcoded version of gender mainstreaming, gender becomes synonymous for "woman" and thus ties women's disenfranchisement to her biology and not to the wider contexts and interpretations of biology. Wolfensohn's story reflects the public face of the World Bank and thus reflects gender mainstreaming policies on this scale.

GENDER MAINSTREAMING AS BEHAVIOR NORMALIZATION

The story of Sonyona Zhanazarova, the Development Project for Indigenous or Afro-Ecuador (commonly known as PRODEPINE in World Bank reports), and development reports on gender mainstreaming worldwide are material examples of the World Bank's "successful" gender mainstreaming initiatives that responded to Wolfensohn's call in 1997. Likewise, the U.S. Personal Responsibility Act reflects the ways that gender mainstreaming ideologies entered a national policy. The rhetoric of gender mainstreaming is transcoded in different ways depending upon geopolitical scale and locale. Looking at World Bank development projects alongside the enrollment of the U.S. Personal Responsibility Act shows that although gender mainstreaming comes to carry neoliberal connotations that focus on changing individual behaviors over a structural and contextual networked analysis of poverty, how women ought to be changed depends upon neocolonial and deeply seated stereotypes about normalcy and not the widespread global political, environmental, and economic changes the Beijing Platform names and recognizes.

The World Bank's implementation of gender mainstreaming policies, alongside the simultaneous global decline of the welfare state, is an example of inextricably linked yet incongruous gender mainstreaming rhetorics. These programs and policies both concentrate on making women materially responsible for their families' own economic situation; however, the Personal Responsibility Act urges single mothers to marry—to become normative global citizens who both fit within and extend gender roles. The Personal Responsibility Act attempts to produce individual citizens whose bodies and sexualities are contained so that they can be productive workers, while the Bank policies attempt to empower women through microeconomic development alongside teaching male partners to participate in household labor (a concept I explore further in chapter 4).

Popular representations of women from the Global South stereotypically characterize these women as being in need of emancipation by the First World from oppressive gender cultural norms; as Gayatri Spivak notes, they tend to be represented as needing to be saved "from brown men."[5] In contrast, U.S. women are often represented as free, autonomous, and liberated subjects unattached to patriarchal structures. Although the policy depictions I explore below may appear to be paradoxical, both sets of policies portray poor women as "backward" or, in the words of Wolfensohn, "unfit." The Personal Responsibility Act represents women as needing to be more integrated into patriarchal structures by becoming proper mothers and wives in a capitalist economy, at once caring and accountable wives and mothers and responsible and productive workers. World Bank development programs, in contrast, recommend that Third World women be taught to be capitalist entrepreneurs who are economically independent of their family, husbands, and sometimes even their community. These gender mainstreaming plans reflect processes of normalization and are part of extending neoliberal nation-state governmentality to global governmentality. Ultimately, both World Bank development initiatives and U.S. welfare policy concentrate on changing women's behaviors and ways of being so that they better fit their nation's (and the globe's) economic needs. These policies transcode gender mainstreaming rhetorics to reflect neoliberal economic ideologies and reflect the U.S. ideology that one must pull oneself up by the bootstraps while also promoting individual economic independence.

For example, the Personal Responsibility Act emphasizes that personal tenacity and engaging in paid labor is the primary way for women to be mainstreamed into the national and global economy. It also focuses on how poor people need to be changed (i.e., managed) in order to be viable in a neoliberal economy. U.S. welfare policies prior to the Personal

Responsibility Act did not center so much on changing behavior as on "supporting" families. The welfare bills throughout the 1970s and 1980s were titled the Family Assistance Act, Family Support Act, and Aid to Families with Dependent Children Act. In these titles, *aid*, *support*, and *assistance* contrast with the Personal Responsibility Act's fixation on *personal responsibility* and illustrate how neoliberalism has shaped how policy makers craft welfare policy arguments. Historically, welfare policy was a sustaining policy, but as the new title (and policy itself) demonstrates, policy makers shift their emphasis toward a policy that attempts to change recipients so that they might be financially independent while having their sexuality and intimate relationships managed at the same time. In this way, the World Bank gender mainstreaming policies and Personal Responsibility Act share a common rhetoric of gender mainstreaming that comes to promote the normalization of individuals. These earlier welfare policies reflect liberal democratic notions of supporting women (albeit in often problematic ways). However, gender mainstreaming in the Personal Responsibility Act transcodes so that it means women supporting and saving themselves without any of the social structures that the Beijing Platform suggests might make this possible, and at the same time they are being managed because they are being "encouraged" to get married. In this way, gender mainstreaming rhetorics become transcoded to fit the United States' context. A transnational feminist rhetorical analysis must illuminate these networked policy arguments about women's place in the global economy by considering how context and place create uneven and sometimes contradictory representations of women.

The Personal Responsibility Act begins by centering on how single motherhood and out-of-wedlock pregnancies are the causes of women's poverty and thus "very important Government interests" (Personal Responsibility and Work Opportunity Reconciliation Act of 1996 101[10]). Accordingly, the policy identifies women's role in maintaining her family's economic security. In the policy, the terms *marriage*, *work*, and *self-sufficiency* emerge as part of the discourse of gender mainstreaming. Consider, as I do in chapter 1, the following statement: "The Congress makes the following findings: (1) Marriage is the foundation of a successful society. (2) Marriage is an essential institution of a successful society which promotes the interest of children" (101[1]). In this example, the

Personal Responsibility Act transcodes the rhetoric of gender mainstreaming to mean managing intimate relationships—this sort of management of private relations will also be examined below in a World Bank gender mainstreaming initiative. The policy continues to describe the dangers of single motherhood: "The negative consequences of an out-of-wedlock birth on the mother, the child, the family, and society are well documented as follows: Children born out-of-wedlock have a substantially higher risk of being born at a low or moderately low birth weight [and] . . . are more likely to have lower cognitive scores, lower educational aspirations" (101[8]). The Personal Responsibility Act references connections between things such as birth weight, cognition, and education and, as such, draws upon deeply historic eugenic ideologies from the early part of the twentieth century. During this time period poor people were thought to be genetically inferior and morally "backward" and essentially unable to become "normal" and productive citizens. While the welfare act of 1996 does not refer to genetics, it does suggest that single and poor women are unfit to be mothers and that only through their ties with men can they produce healthy children. Essentially, the policy argues that to make women viable in this new economy they must create state-sanctioned, heteronormative, two-parent family alliances. Yet, the Beijing Platform specifically recognizes the importance of gender mainstreaming initiatives that support a variety of family structures: two-parent, single-parent, multigenerational, and even multispoused families (see *Beijing Declaration* 12; chapter 4 of this book).

While, as I demonstrate below, the World Bank gender mainstreaming policies focus on making women entrepreneurs by providing microloans, the U.S. policy turns to the traditional two-parent heterosexual home as part of their transcoded rhetoric of gender mainstreaming. However, because of the United States' neoliberal context, where social services for the poor have been drastically reduced and middle-class wages, due to de-industrialization, have all but disappeared, making single-earner households a rarity, women must also *work* outside the home. To make this point clear, the policy describes how women should "transition from economic dependency to self-sufficiency through work" (Personal Responsibility and Work Opportunity Reconciliation Act of 1996 817[c]); the policy lists an extensive set of statistics that show how two-parent married and two-parent working families are less likely to be impoverished and less likely to use welfare services (see 101[1–10]). In this welfare policy, men only come into focus as husbands or fathers, but there is not a move to change men's behaviors or ontologies; instead the policy suggests that *women* must be self-sufficient and responsible, suggesting that they are not already. Interestingly, men's role in the home and their traditional gender role are not looked at as a problem. So, for example, in the United States many women bear the burden of double workdays and work full time inside and outside the home in formal labor. Many men also work formally outside the home, but they are not expected to become more responsible for housework, for instance.[6] In the U.S. context, gender mainstreaming then moves away from nations and supranations saving women (something I explore more closely in chapter 4) and instead focuses on teaching women to manage themselves, their homes, and their formal labor. Controlling women's sexuality in the interest of exploiting their labor (here, labor that is done outside the home rather than just reproductive labor) is ultimately a form of patriarchy, which the Beijing Platform clearly identifies as one of the key hurdles women face.

In contrast, some World Bank gender mainstreaming initiatives do focus on women *and* men, and yet, like the U.S. Personal Responsibility Act, these initiatives also transcode gender mainstreaming to mean changing ontologies and behaviors. In Ecuador, the World Bank development program PRODEPINE also focused on making women entrepreneurs. Through the loan, the women were leased stoves upon which they were to cook food for commercial sale, even though through interviews (see Bedford) the women explicitly stated that they needed health and child care to help them with their labor. Like the U.S. Personal Responsibility Act, then, the program centers on making women better workers outside the home and men more responsible caretakers inside the home. A World Bank review document called *Ecuador Gender Review*, which describes the successes and failures of the loan in terms of gender mainstreaming initiatives, begins with a seemingly nuanced understanding, reflective of the Beijing Platform and of the constraints to gender mainstreaming, it states: "Macro-economic crises have gendered impacts, with women tending to enter into the labor force during these periods. This implies greater pressures on their time given that adjustments in the division of household work have not taken place. For men, unemployment threatens their role of family provider and creates problems of self esteem and depression —which may have other possible negative effects such as violence" (x). In response, however, the Bank staff in charge of the loan and program focused on the socialization processes that reinforce traditional gender roles, noting that "gender roles, stereotypes and expectations can influence the opportunities men and women have and the constraints they face as well as their choices and decisions over their lifetime. Ultimately, rigid gender roles can negatively affect socialization, . . . girls are expected to work in the home, where they are less likely to gain human capital and which, in turn, influences their labor market opportunities and earning potential later in life" (*Ecuador Gender Review* xi–xii).

The Bank staff created gender socialization materials—in which ironically, as Kate Bedford notes, each chapter began with a quote from Lacanian psychoanalysis Franciose Dolto who writes about love and its ability to unite men and women—that worked to "promote men's roles as fathers and caregivers, particularly among unemployed men" because "men are often underemployed or off work during economic downturns and therefore could share the burden of household responsibilities. In contrast, women often enter the workforce to compensate for household income losses during periods of economic crisis and have less time to engage in domestic chores" (*Ecuador Gender Review* xiii; 57). Unlike the U.S. welfare policy, this World Bank loan focuses on gender mainstreaming as being important for both men and women; in this case, gender mainstreaming means teaching men to perform different duties than they typically would perform. Yet as Bedford points out in her exploration of the loan and through her on-the-ground work, the Bank staff also depicted men as lazy, drunken, and unfaithful infidels. Thus, much of the loan focused on teaching men to be proper husbands, despite the fact that the women the loan targeted did not complain about the men's behaviors. If the colonialist discourse "saves" brown women from brown men, neocolonialist discourse "manages" brown men so they won't get in the way of brown women's ability to contribute to the formal economy.

Just as the loan targets men's behaviors, it also notes how traditional gender roles and gendered opportunities impact women's well-being. While the report attempts to reflect the Beijing Platform's definition of gender mainstreaming by making reference to the fact that women and men in Ecuador must follow seemingly limited and rigid gender roles, it shifts the definition away from the platform's holistic understanding of the vectors of oppression that women face (the Beijing Platform also notes, as I mention above, how gender role expectations might differ from class to class, region to region). The reference to "human capital" demonstrates how this gender mainstreaming initiative transcodes the term so that it references neoliberal labor expectations, therefore making women workers in a global capitalist economy.

As established above, the World Bank and U.S. policy makers both concentrate on paid out-of-home work for women; yet this focus produces a material conundrum: because policy makers give so much attention to getting women into the paid labor force, they must consider women's unpaid labor of raising children and maintaining their household (Bedford 295). The means by which each policy deals with unpaid care work shows how gender logics become transcoded as the logic crosses national and developmental boundaries. In the United States, for example, the Personal Responsibility Act legislates that "needy families [must make a plan] so that children may be cared for in their own homes or in the homes of relatives" (Personal Responsibility and Work Opportunity Reconciliation Act of 1996 401[a]). This portion of the welfare act ties women back to traditional institutions like the family and reasserts a transcoded gender mainstreaming rhetoric that individual families must take care of each other and are thus not the state's responsibility. This rhetoric contrasts strongly with the World Bank's plans, which stress how market activities create new labor demands that can enable women to work outside the home and be less dependent upon their families—just as men become more responsible for their families (i.e., assuming that men are not responsible in the first place). To deal with the conundrum of unpaid and in-home labor, the World Bank recommends a classed division of labor, whereby some women hire other women to provide care work and other women are hired to do that care work.

The 2001 gender mainstreaming World Bank report, *Engendering Development through Gender Equity in Rights, Resources, and Voice*, a follow up to the report *Toward Gender Equality*, also specifically address women's issues such as care work. Both are accounts of the results of Wolfensohn's plans for "inclusion." Like the Personal Responsibility Act, *Engendering Development* frames its arguments for gender mainstreaming around the terms *rights*, *resources*, and *voice*, linking the report's overarching argument to the neoliberal ideologies of agency, autonomy, and personal responsibility. The report's argument depicts Third World women as excessively bound to their cultural norms. Following a discourse of neoliberalism, *Engendering Development* argues that the best way to emancipate Third World women from binding traditional ties is to "include" them in the capitalist market mainstream. Yet, unlike the Personal Responsibility Act, which ties women back to traditional institutions like the home and family, *Engendering Development* suggests that women's subordination is tied to traditional work and a lack of contact with modern institutions and markets; these modern institutions and markets will enable women to work outside the home while their families are cared for by other women.

Toward Gender Equality, a World Bank publication from 1995, likewise explains how social norms (including community ties and traditional familial relationships) are a hindrance to macro-level economic development: "Social norms affecting decisions within the family about occupational choices or migration can also lead to differential patterns of male and female earnings in informal markets. Family responsibilities hinder women's geographic mobility, constraining their ability to command high wages" (34). Both reports suggest that if women had access to credit and earned wages, then they could have more bargaining power within the home and the community; this money would create financial and cultural equality between men and women. *Engendering Development* explains: "Women who participate in the credit programs report an increased role in household decision making and greater acceptance by their husbands of their participation in market-based economic activities" (164). In other words, the Bank suggests that gender inequality is not only bad for women but that it also "hinders [the] development" of her nation (73); women, therefore, are key resources for the global economy. The World Bank's rhetoric of gender mainstreaming is that the availability of credit and markets will save women from what the Bank describes as oppressive traditional or "unfit" ways of being. The word *unfit* ties a gendered individual body to an economic system. The Bank ultimately wants to produce "fit" workers.

This transcoded neoliberal gender mainstreaming rhetoric that credit and markets empower women is enabled by gendered colonial discourses. For example, in a World Bank informational pamphlet the audience is introduced to a woman named Sonyona Zhanazarova, or "Sonya," from the Kyrgyz Republic:

> Unable to afford a stall in the produce hall, [Zhanazarova] sold pistachios from a small table outside the building—even during freezing months—until she banded together with 11 other women to form a village banking group. Hoping to find the capital to help grow her business, Sonya turned to the Foundation for International Community Assistance (FINCA), a provider of tiny loans to poor entrepreneurs, which is supported by the World Bank's private-sector arm, the International Finance Corporation. A $40 loan allowed Sonya to buy more pistachios and begin expanding her own business. (*World Bank Group* 1)

This narrative highlights attributes that make a citizen successful in a neoliberal economy: tenacity, personal responsibility, and individualism. As the story explains, Zhanazarova "banded together" with other women and then sought out and found financing for her business. Unlike conventional stories of Third World women's empowerment, Zhanazarova is not seen as a victim, but instead she is characterized as an active entrepreneur —an emblem of women's economic empowerment. Such neoliberal logic suggests that women like Zhanazarova are disenfranchised not by their material conditions or locale but by their own lack of will. I do not doubt that the loan provided to Zhanazarova was helpful; she and her coworkers were able to expand their business. Yet, just as Zhanazarova is empowered by the Bank to obtain financing, her subjectivity is limited by the pamphlet's use of a Westernized diminutive of her name. Reiterating colonial era stories, in the short narrative Sononya Zhanazarova is changed to a Westernized "Sonya" signifying that she has been mainstreamed in the sense that she is recognizable. While the pamphlet's shortening of her name might invite audiences (particularly English-speaking members) to identify with her, the act erases the material circumstances Zhanazarova faces. "Sonya," the self-sufficient entrepreneur, is further accessible as the good "Westernized" neocolonial other by the pamphlet's depiction of her as empowered to make the right choices. The neocolonial story has distinct resonance for a Western audience: the narrative shifts gender mainstreaming away from considering material constraints and instead privileges individualism. The Bank portrays Zhanazarova's choices as a key marker of successful gender mainstreaming initiatives.

Zhanazarova's story may mimic typical colonial representations, but neoliberalism transcodes the meaning of gender mainstreaming, signaled by her embracing the values of tenacity and self-sufficiency in order to be successful in the new economy. Like the World Bank's report on a gender mainstreaming project in Ecuador and in the U.S. Personal Responsibility Act, which also attempts to change the person (and culture) a policy addresses, in this success story, Zhanazarova not only has her name changed to reflect her subjectivity in this new economy but her business has been mainstreamed into the economy as well. The loan that she received must be paid back (usually with interest, something that I explore further in chapter 4) to service the company or organization that invested in her. Nonetheless, in this story of Zhanazarova, gender mainstreaming becomes part of the rhetoric of neoliberalism in the sense that through the process of owning and running a business Zhanazarova becomes an independent entrepreneur who appears to not need social or governmental intervention. While the Beijing Platform recommends that nations support women in their work inside and outside the home through strong social services alongside listening directly to women's voices and their needs, this story demonstrates development as unidirectional. This illustrates a remarkable shift away from a networked understanding of women's oppression put forth in the Beijing Platform.

The World Bank's *Engendering Development* further transcodes and connects gender mainstreaming to neoliberal market aims through its definition of women's rights as the ability to "own land, manage property, conduct business, or . . . travel without their husband's consent" (4). These basic rights that the report defines are indeed important, but they also resonate strongly with Westernized notions of sovereignty and individualism and stereotypical colonial understandings of Third World women. The terms *own*, *manage*, and *business* demonstrate a revised rhetoric of gender mainstreaming that works with neoliberal ideologies because the terms emphasize personal tenacity and entrepreneurialism (something I also address further in chapter 4). The final clause of that list, "travel without their husband's consent," however, disrupts these entrepreneurial aims. While it is certainly positive for women to travel independently, this short list shows how neoliberal arguments work in tandem with and are dependent upon neocolonial ideologies—essentially, the assumption that women from poor countries have limited mobility and that this limited mobility hiders the development of markets and economies. *Engendering Development* continues: "Gender disparities in rights constrain the sets of choices available to women in many aspects of life—often profoundly limiting their ability to participate in or benefit from development" (4). The Bank reads cultural practices according to (and into) the logic of the market. In these examples gender mainstreaming rhetorics are transcoded so that cultural context is discarded in favor of the personal and (inter)national economic mobility that the market enables.

A section called, "Fostering Economic Development to Strengthen Incentives for More Equal Resources and Participation," in *Engendering Development* further demonstrates how the Bank transcodes the rhetoric of gender mainstreaming away from the Beijing Platform; it states: "where active labor markets exist, hired labor provides a substitute for female family labor, whether on farms or in household maintenance or care activities. This allows households to use time more efficiently, perhaps reducing women's workload. Where labor markets are absent or do not function well, such substitution is not possible" (19). This statement exemplifies an important contradiction in the Bank's gender mainstreaming rhetoric. When markets are present they provide the opportunity for women, but such opportunities may only benefit some women—to the extent that they can hire other women—and thus enter into a classed capitalist system.

Unlike the U.S. context, where care work becomes a family's responsibility, according to this plan Third World women entrust care work to the market. Yet, neither of these plans have women's best interests in mind. The World Bank suggests that women hire other women without accounting for the fact that only a certain class of women can hire other women to provide in-home care. Likewise, the Personal Responsibility Act's mandate that children be cared for in their own homes assumes that at least one adult member of a household does not work. Within many poor families even senior-citizen members of a multigenerational household often work outside the home. This care work conundrum exhibits the faulty logic of these transcoded neoliberal gender mainstreaming policies and shows that state support may be necessary for a family's survival.

As these examples make clear, gender mainstreaming rhetorics shift and change as they cross national and developmental boundaries because relations of power and context impact communicative policy networks and thus the ways in which policy portrays women as economic actors. According to the Beijing Platform, gender mainstreaming is only possible by understanding how women's well-being relates to wider contexts such as structural adjustment, war, post- and neocolonialism and stereotypical representations of women; however, the Personal Responsibility and Work Opportunity Reconciliation Act of 1996 argues that U.S. women must be core economic actors and thus become better workers and better mothers who are more attached to their families, while according to the World Bank's "The Challenge of Inclusion," and World Bank programs like those in Ecuador, Third World women should de-emphasize family attachments by leaving behind their "traditional" role as mothers and wives so that they can become thriving entrepreneurs.

These public policy arguments link First and Third World women by portraying women simultaneously as individual earners and producers for the global economy and demonstrate how gender mainstreaming rhetorics can be malleable and then transcoded. World Bank gender mainstreaming policies and U.S. welfare policies contain appeals to neoliberal ideologies of rights, choice, and individual agency and also promote neoliberal governmentalities. Yet, both policy arguments rhetorically and materially interpolate women within a capitalist economy—a system reliant upon class and, in this case, gender stratification. Importantly, as the Beijing Platform addresses, gender mainstreaming policies cannot see *all* women as having the same desires and interests; rather, the Beijing Platform networks women's interests to their wider contexts. These documents represent women as a singular class with similar aspirations—or at least that they ought to have similar aspirations. In this document, their "desire and interest" (Spivak 258) do not coincide—in their daily lives, even when these lives involve significant risk and danger, women do not identify as a class. The transcoded neoliberal narrative of gender mainstreaming attempts to change women's behavior and shift women's dependency from the state to the market (and ultimately to the global capitalist economy) while heightening gender stratification by making women primarily responsible for their poor families. Although different, U.S. welfare policies and the World Bank's gender mainstreaming policies share an understanding of gender mainstreaming that is drastically different from the Beijing Platform and suggests that material inequalities can be overcome by managing women's actions.

■ ■ ■ ■ ■

GENDER mainstreaming rhetorics are transcoded to be part of a neoliberal and neocolonial discourse and to fit different argument platforms. Networking gender mainstreaming arguments across several documents enables rhetoricians to examine how, through the process of transcoding, contemporary policy arguments always become entangled in larger historical relationships of power and how these arguments get reinterpreted and rewritten during economic shifts and changes such as those brought about during the rise of neoliberal economics. The Beijing Platform ultimately suggests that women of all backgrounds must be active in the creation of public policies so that the policies reflect their needs; it says for example that "women/gender units are important for effective mainstreaming, but strategies must be further developed to prevent inadvertent marginalization as opposed to mainstreaming of the gender dimension throughout all operations" (122). Yet, post Beijing the World Bank employs archetypical colonial discourses that render women "underdeveloped" and thus in need of being saved by the capitalist economy, while the U.S. Personal Responsibility Act similarly depicts welfare-using women as "backward": amoral and unmarried and physically, mentally, and cognitively harming their children. Because the World Bank represents women as powerless and sometimes even "primitive," they illustrate that investors and development experts need to create policy interventions that would make women viable entrepreneurs. Likewise the U.S. welfare act argues that to prepare women for the neoliberal economy the policy must attempt to make women better caregivers inside and workers outside the home through the institution of marriage. However, unlike the United States' welfare policy, which focused on ending poverty by promoting financial independence from the state through marriage and kinship ties, the World Bank's gender mainstreaming policies focus on making women *less* accountable to their familial and community ties and more responsible for their own personal economic independence. These examples demonstrate rhetorical transcoding—how rhetorics shift as they move from document to document, from scale to scale—noting specifically how policy makers argue that to make welfare recipients and Third World women viable economic actors they must be fundamentally changed. In short, within these policies, the meaning of gender mainstreaming shifts away from the broader contexts of poverty, embraces a neoliberal understanding of poverty, and, as a result, focuses on individual behaviors.

By networking gender mainstreaming arguments across documents and exploring how policy makers and development experts transcode gender mainstreaming from a term that describes a holistic process of considering the vectors of women's oppression to a term that unites neocolonial ideologies with neoliberal economic plans, feminist rhetoricians can decipher the rhetorics that ultimately support global governmentality—that is, how the gender mainstreaming rhetorics have material effects and thus impact the ways women are managed. By noting how rhetorics are transcoded, I have also tracked the way policies create gendered workers, specifically how women are constituted as a class (even though they might not see themselves this way) legislated to act in particular ways.

These material effects impact which women's voices are heard, how they are represented, in what situation their words are used, and when they are allowed to speak. Looking at how rhetorics move, how rhetorics sometimes carry residual ideologies (such as colonial and neoliberal ideologies, as I explore here), and how such ideologies might be recuperated, I offer feminist rhetoricians an examination of the preconditions and pretexts for understanding the circumstances within which women can speak (or are allowed to speak and be heard), and in doing so I also offer a concrete example of how gendered *global* governmentality works. In the policies and development initiatives I explore here, women's actual needs and voices disappear in the translation of gender mainstreaming from the Beijing Platform into a neoliberal ideology that states that when women are brought into a mainstream market and formal economy, they become free. Before marginalized voices can be recovered, before audiences can be moved to action, we need to understand networked power and transcoded rhetorics by paying attention to how the process of moving texts from one scale to another may have the effect of *further* silencing women. Ultimately, paying attention to rhetorical transcoding brings awareness to the wider contexts that enable some discourse on and about women to circulate and others not. In this way, I also offer feminist recovery efforts a rich and specific examination of power as it works in various contexts, linking to neocolonial discourses and neoliberal economics. By looking beyond the instruments of policy making and beyond individual rhetorical acts, feminist rhetoricians can link contexts with how policies and development plans represent certain people and then also how political and policy issues are rhetorically constructed.

3 FITNESS

In this chapter, I trace the rhetorics of fitness between three texts, a World Bank promotional and informational pamphlet and the disability and development films *From Exclusion to Inclusion* and *A World Enabled*, which I encountered at a single occasion (a two-day World Bank conference on disability in 2004). By performing a transnational feminist rhetorical analysis of these texts that networks ideologies across time, the past is made visible by unpacking the palimpsest discursive layers that support rhetorical terms and arguments. As presented in chapter 2, the Beijing Platform networked gender mainstreaming arguments to a variety of contexts, noting that women's well-being could not simply be measured by economics. Post Beijing, however, policy makers transcoded gender mainstreaming rhetorics to carry neoliberal connotations; as a result, gender mainstreaming came to mean "fitting" women into a global capitalist economy by changing their behaviors.

Wolfensohn's speech in 1997, "The Challenge of Inclusion," then evokes this very notion of fitness or "fitting in"; and, as this chapter will further demonstrate through an analysis of documents coming out of a World Bank conference, it also brings to mind some of the political and social ideologies of the early twentieth century in the United States. During this time policy makers and social activists, seeking to solidify U.S. national identity, wanted to create the industrialized normal citizen-worker. Not only were these workers, through invariable physical fitness and productivity, supposed to maintain their nation's fitness, their "fit" and standardized bodies would preserve their country's economic "fitness." The fit body would be able to perform the tasks necessary for factory work and goods production—the necessities for building a strong national economy. The "unfit abnormal body," however, during industrialization, was relegated to the welfare system because it could not literally work (Davis 40). To some extent then, the words *unfit* and *fit* evoke the discourse of normal citizenship and even eugenics (and Darwin's theory of the survival of the fittest), reminding North American audiences of height and weight charts, psychological testing, the classification of ability, and the building of a national citizenry and economy. In the context of globalization and transnational capital, making the unfit fit then means not only making the citizen body fit for work but also making the nation fit into a global economy.

Wolfensohn's rhetoric of fitness (as well as many post-Beijing gender mainstreaming documents) implies an erasure of difference as it discounts non-Western or other forms of (informal) economic viability and other forms of bodily viability. Thus, the rhetorical appeal of fitness rests upon the audience's desire to comprehend or make "normal" a country's economic, social, and governmental practices—another form of global governmentality where bodies and economies are uniformly managed. In this formula, "all working bodies are equal to all other working bodies because they are interchangeable . . . all citizens must have standard bodies to be able to fit into the industrial-political notion of democracy, equality, and normality" (Davis, *Bending* 111). In Wolfensohn's speech, by making "developing" nations fit into what he describes as the "mainstream," countries are given the task of maintaining the "normative" function of the global economy and ultimately of stratifying nations that are fit and unfit. Likewise, individual citizens of these developing nations must support their nation's globalized economy by entering into the capitalist market and producing commodities that will demarcate their acquiescence of "normal" economic activity. This sort of discourse of normalcy is reified when the state—or another governing body such as a supranational organization—attempts to make "normal" those who are deemed as unfit, nonstandard, or incomprehensible (Davis, *Enforcing Normalcy* 30).

As a result, Wolfensohn's rhetoric of fitness resonates with modern conceptualizations of "normality," whereby individuals practice moderation, discretion, diligence, and moral self-improvement (Terry 11), and neoliberal renditions, whereby people are responsible for their own economic behaviors. Without such self-regulation, the "abnormal" or non-mainstream is a threat to the security of those who appear to have embraced normality, whether through personal practices and behaviors or through nation-state development processes and governing. Crucially, however, as Rosemarie Garland-Thomson points out, "the disabled body exposes the illusion of autonomy, self-government, and self-determination that underpins the fantasy of absolute able-bodiedness" and, as I show in this chapter, neoliberal ideologies (*Extraordinary Bodies* 46).

Ironically, seven years after the World Bank's formal agreement to practice gender mainstreaming and then soon after employing development policies that ultimately sought to change people to make them "fit," the World Bank held a conference on disability and development, "Disability and Inclusive Development: Sharing, Learning and Building Alliances," at their headquarters in Washington, D.C. I attended this conference in hopes of seeing international policy making in action. Sitting in a crowded, standing room only lecture hall, I listened as Wolfensohn welcomed us to the conference. Referring to his commitment to gender mainstreaming, his opening speech first reminded his audience that recently, "gender was an issue that was . . . given a backward place until [the Bank] discovered that the key to development was, in fact, women" ("Disability and Development"). Wolfensohn then suggested it was time for the Bank to similarly bring a disability perspective to all levels of development.

To some extent, I believe it is important that the World Bank devotes projects, programs, and development monies to address the needs of women and people with disabilities because these two groups do tend to be most vulnerable to poverty worldwide. However, Wolfensohn's performative speech, which reiterated harrowing statistics and stories about people with disabilities across the world, demonstrates the need for some sort of intervention, and his representation of "the disabled" global citizen relies upon audience members' preconceived notions and visual expectations about Third World "backwardness" and "the disabled's" victimhood —both part of pretext and discourse of normalcy. In this speech Wolfensohn demonstrates how historic ideologies about disability and normalcy can traffic in new constructions of ability that displace economic interests and objectives onto the bodies of people with disabilities.

In Wolfensohn's rhetoric of fitness, we can detect what M. Jacqui Alexander refers to as "ideological trafficking"—rhetorical "formations that are otherwise positioned as dissimilar" because of the fact that they might appear within a wholly different time, place, or situation (190). Ideological traffic draws attention to history—of rhetorical actors, of rhetorics that have long circulated, and of the occasions when these actors and rhetorics emerge. Tracing ideological traffic enables rhetoricians to identify and analyze which rhetorical terms are glossed over or taken for granted because they have circulated without question for decades and thus have become ingrained and common sense. Homi Bhabha, when talking about how and why colonial images and ideologies tend to circulate over and over, without question, describes these as ambivalent discourses and in doing so draws attention to how representations have material power (especially as these very discourses are used to create arguments for global policy initiatives that may reorganize people's lives and livelihoods) and affects when audiences do not notice them since they are so commonplace. Following ideological traffic and networking taken-for-granted and historical arguments within a single occasion lays bare the rhetorics that have become naturalized and a common part of our political imaginary.

We see this sort of ideological trafficking in Wolfensohn's speech as he reaches back to employ terms from the early part of the twentieth century and in its movement for social hygiene (fit, unfit, and backward); such discourses are so deeply ingrained that they can be difficult to "see" or analyze. Given that Wolfenoshn, at this conference, intertextually references his speech on gender mainstreaming from 1997, whereby he describes the Bank as working to make "the unfit fit," and due to the context of the disability speech (and the overarching goals of the World Bank's development projects), we can note ideological trafficking by making connections between these speeches and dominant discourses on ability and normativity. Yet, the disabled body at once shores up and disrupts ideological traffic. Such bodies are contradictory for neoliberal development because they inherently expose how the notion of choice, personal responsibility, and individual will is not always possible.

This chapter demonstrates another form of a transnational feminist rhetorical analysis, as I consider the ideological traffic in the World Bank's rhetoric of fitness by looking at how arguments are networked across histories and to happenings seemingly outside of a semiclosed rhetorical situation—a single occasion. In doing so, I use *occasion* in three ways: to mean a particular time, a chance or opportunity, and a cause or reason. I look at how arguments are networked within a single occasion to show that ideologies traffic across time and texts. I also illustrate how rhetoricians can perform a transnational feminist analysis without having to follow rhetorics from one rhetorical situation to another. A transnational feminist rhetorical lens can also help elucidate how, within a single occasion, we can read the wider histories and contexts that traffic within arguments about women and people with disabilities across the globe. Ultimately, I point out how a single occasion can be an exigency for rhetorics to shift and change.

Accordingly, I show ideological trafficking in two ways. First, I present how rhetoricians can see "the old" (in this case normalizing and colonial discourses) structured through what looks like new and progressive polices (here, development plans for people with disabilities) (Alexander 189–91). Alexander notes the importance of transnational feminists reading across time and space in order to notice how seemingly "material boundaries [often] dovetail with imperatives that are . . . closely aligned with . . . colonization," for example (189), and also how "different narrations [over] time . . . [can] unravel that which has been normalized and normativized [as] homogenous" (191). Second, I extend Alexander's notion of ideological trafficking to look, through a transnational feminist lens, at rhetorics across a single occasion. Keeping with her theory of looking across spaces to see how discourses (or in my case rhetorics) shift, change, or stay the same, I consider what happens when there is ideological traffic within a single occasion, especially when two groups are talking about the same thing (helping people with disabilities), but in doing so they expose each other's material limitations.

Using ideological trafficking as a transnational feminist rhetorical analytic, I read tropes of fitness as first neoliberal normativity in texts that present themselves as working against such normalizing discourses: the very documents produced by the World Bank for the 2004 disability conference. Yet, I also see, in a film shown at the conference and produced by disability activist Victor Pineda, how ideological trafficking can be unraveled as the film exposes the contradictions in the World Bank's rhetoric of fitness and the limitations of neoliberal notions of work and autonomy, calling instead for making the world more fit for all bodies by emphasizing agency through adaptive technologies and universal design. While Pineda's film demonstrates that development is a necessity for many lower-income nations, it proposes another form of development that does not merely promote formal laboring activities as fitness; instead the film suggests that development experts use their resources to make *fit environments.*

In this single occasion, I examine how these competing and contradictory rhetorics of fitness traffic between World Bank documents and disability activists' documents and then trace how these competing and contradictory rhetorics of fitness converge with each other in postconference disability and development initiatives and, in doing so, redefine fitness. I see the World Bank conference as what Antonio Gramsci calls a conjunctural moment where contradictions become visible and when the discursive relationships that construct a historical moment become clear. As Rachel Reidner and Kevin Mahoney note, during conjunctural moments new activist responses are possible (see *Democracies to Come*).

Transnational feminists seek to locate nodes of power in unexpected places and in doing so pay particular attention to history as it is influenced by shifts in the global economy, state-to-state relationships, and even activist organizing. Activist discourses are typically seen as marginal in a center and periphery model of organization; however, transnational feminist analytics seek to muddle the notion that only the center has power, and instead they look to alternative spaces to find counter-hegemonies. Bringing together activist and supranational institutions, as I do here, disrupts this traditional way of locating power.[1] Likewise, disability scholars and activists have been at the forefront of not only demonstrating the links between the center and the periphery but working against neoliberal notions of individualism and self-sovereignty.[2] They have also challenged the view that disability is an *individual* defect that can be fixed either through medical intervention or science. In doing so, they have exposed how people are intimately reliant upon other people (whether disabled or not) and upon economic structures and policies for survival. Scholars such as Rosemarie Garland-Thompson, Lennard Davis, and Simi Linton, for example, note instead how political, economic, cultural, and geopolitical factors impact how disability is framed and addressed; they also note that disability is only a disability due to environmental infrastructures and deeply seated ideologies about people with disabilities that stem as far back as Aristotle and as more recent as the early twentieth-century eugenics movement. Of late, the field of disability studies has noted that, due to contemporary globalization and its resulting economic and social policies, disability must be placed in a broad transnational context (see, for example, a *Disability Studies Quarterly* special issue on disability and human rights in 2009). They make clear what Anthony Giddens notes: that in a neoliberal economy the welfare state or any state dependence is seen as a weakness or a disability because it exposes the inherent contradiction of the notion of self-reliance for citizens (13).

By following ideological trafficking then, I also bring a disability studies lens to transnational feminist theory by examining how notions of bodily and ontological normalcy circulate, appear, and are challenged within developmental discourse. In addition, tracing ideological traffic also helps feminist rhetoricians network arguments to larger histories and ideologies (such as eugenics and colonial expectations), thereby also enabling them not only to critique discourses but also to conceptualize the material results of rhetorics.

In this chapter then, transnational feminist rhetorical analysis networks ideologies across time and also makes connections between dissimilar (and competing) arguments. Ultimately, I demonstrate how to bring a transnational feminist rhetorical analysis to a single occasion by connecting rhetorical actors with their multiple yet networked histories.

The first section of this chapter analyzes the World Bank's discourse of normalcy as it is employed in their promotional pamphlet *World Bank Group: Working for a World Free of Poverty*, which I received at the conference, in order to show the ideological traffic that informs the ways in which the World Bank (unwittingly) represents itself as a normalizing institution. Tracing ideological traffic is important for understanding the contradictions in the World Bank's claim that they want to support people with disabilities across the globe.

Despite the World Bank's attempt, beginning in 1997 with gender mainstreaming, to make the "unfit fit," the very development plans it promotes depends upon an illusive standardized, homogenized, and normalized body politic that reinforces the exact problems that the Bank purports to address (Davis, *Bending Over Backwards*; Hahn; and Garland-Thomson, *Extraordinary Bodies*). The rhetoric of fitness that the Bank puts forth in this pamphlet relies upon and furthers representations of colonial "backwardness" while also maintaining and reifying historic discourses of normalcy and able-bodied global citizenship. The Bank's larger neocolonial and neoliberal project, as the pamphlet depicts, rhetorically constructs nations, citizens, and the global community as having universal goals and fundamental similarities that aid entry into normative economic processes. These very economic arguments remarginalize people with disabilities by reinforcing "such concepts as will, ability, progress, responsibility, and free agency" (Garland-Thomson, *Extraordinary Bodies* 47)—the very neoliberal ideologies that the body with a disability may not be able to live out.[3] Because the Bank pamphlet represents Third World subjectivity as "backward," "unfit," and ultimately outside the mainstream of (capitalist) economic development, development practitioners or policy makers at the conference may have been persuaded to act because this representation renders lower-income nations and people as disorganized, not controlled, and incomprehensible. Bringing the "backward" into the mainstream of economic development produces coherent, controllable, organized, and ultimately safe populations and manageable workers.

The second part of this chapter explores two films with competing rhetorics of fitness that played side-by-side during the conference. In these films, we see how the rhetoric of fitness traffics between films and also shifts and changes; we also see an unspoken contradiction between these films and their producers (both at the conference—one able-bodied and seemingly independent, the other in a wheelchair with his companion along to help him). The World Bank produced the first film and disability activists the second. The first World Bank–produced film, *From Exclusion to Inclusion*, tells the story of accommodation. Julie Jung identifies a similar narrative of accommodation in her exploration of how composition texts present disability; she claims that "accommodation becomes synonymous with 'fitting in,' a definition that locates the responsibility for adaptation within the 'abnormal' body [or through personal agency] rather than within the institutions and ideologies that construct it as such" (130). This notion of personal responsibility for "fitting in" reflects the neoliberal ideologies I explored in chapters 1 and 2, which focused on global governmentality or changing people to fit in with a growing global capitalist economy.

I show how the film *From Exclusion to Inclusion* reproduces rhetorics of fitness that rely upon normalizing discourses that render some disabled bodies (particularly those who reside in high-income nations) as unseen and adapted and others (such as those who appear to come from low-income nations) as both fit and superhuman when they participate in formal and income-earning laboring activities; yet, this representation ignores the lived experience that the film presents. As I describe further below, the film begins with people who work within the administrative portion of the World Bank talking about their disability, but as an audience we only see what appear to be able bodies.

In contrast, the film represents people with *seen* disabilities as either monstrous victims or docile workers. The rhetoric of fitness appears in this film in images that render some people with disabilities as productive and "normal" and others as pathetic, "disfigured" victims. This rhetoric disturbingly traffics colonial discourses and discourses of normalcy and ability. On one level, this film's varying representations of people with disabilities addresses disability scholars such as Harlan Hahn and James C. Wilson and Cynthia Lewiecki-Wilson's concerns, because some of the film images not only objectify or victimize people with disabilities but also show how people with disabilities are productive members of society. At the same time, however, it is significant that the images where people with disabilities appear as victims are also the same people the Bank is working to fit into global capitalism by attempting to transform them from disabled bodies to workers. *From Exclusion to Inclusion* demonstrates ideological trafficking by reflecting a dually historic tendency to portray the physical (and mental) traits of colonized or Third World people *and* people with disabilities as monstrous, uncontrollable, incomprehensible *or* exceedingly docile and genial (see, for example, Hahn; Narayan; and Lutz and Collins).

In contrast, the film *A World Enabled*, by disability activist Victor Pineda, represents a disabling world and in doing so exposes the inherent shortcomings of the World Bank's neoliberal development plans by literally showing how in various low-income countries work programs (as well as welfare programs) have actually marginalized people with disabilities and brought them into greater poverty. The film shows Pineda visiting a variety of countries to see and show (Pineda uses a wheelchair) how people with disabilities survive different economies and governments. Pineda himself, as he navigates various terrains and relies in some cases more and less on his companions and care workers, demonstrates how social stigmas, rehabilitation ideologies, and single-vision economic plans can limit the agency of people with disabilities, what Pineda describes as "personal freedoms." *A*

World Enabled, however, twists the definition of "fitting in" by exposing the limitation of these neoliberal and normative aims and suggesting that the world needs to become more fit for *all* people, thereby delinking an individual person's responsibility for fitting in. Moreover, while *From Exclusion to Inclusion* seeks to accommodate and normalize people with disabilities into working bodies, *A World Enabled* makes the argument that putting people with disabilities to work often re-marginalizes them —by cloistering them in work institutions away from their diverse communities and then also hiding them and their differently functioning bodies away from the public—and does not bring them out of poverty.

The very presence of these two groups at one conference draws attention to the Bank's contradictory rhetoric of fitness because, as *A World Enabled* makes clear, bodies with a disability are obvious markers of the limitations and contradictions of neoliberal ideologies. The final section of this chapter demonstrates a conjunctural moment when contradictions become visible at the conference itself and then produce a counter-hegemonic discourse. I show how both these groups' arguments become networked within a series of supranational guiding documents written after this conference through their reiteration (and a shift in ideological traffic) of fitness. Ultimately, this chapter not only reads how rhetorics of fitness compete during a single rhetorical occasion but also shows how arguments are *always* networked. Even though the two groups of texts I explore (those produced by disability activists and those produced by the World Bank) have different histories, stakes, and exigencies, their rhetorics, because they are framed by a single occasion, are networked.

IDEOLOGICAL TRAFFICKING: NETWORKING DISCOURSES ACROSS TIME

The World Bank's overarching rhetoric of fitness and teleological narrative of development demonstrates how rhetoric traffics with historical discourses of normativity and neoliberal ideologies; this can be seen especially in the promotional pamphlet *World Bank Group: Working for a World Free of Poverty.* While I do not examine how the Bank represents people with disabilities specifically, I suggest that the Bank's overall mission (as communicated in the pamphlet's visual rhetoric) demonstrates a common representational slippage between the "normal" global citizen and the "backward" (disabled) Third World object. I argue that the Bank's visual rhetoric naturalizes the differences between "backward" and disabled countries by imposing a development process that attempts to standardize a country's economic and cultural practices. This argument calls attention to how the Bank's rhetoric traffics with colonial and normalizing discourses as it frames its arguments for "helping the poorest of the poor" (see the World Bank's mission statement).

A transnational feminist rhetorical analysis of the pamphlet's ideological traffic demonstrates the World Bank's less obvious underpinning arguments by focusing on the rhetorical use of colonial human-interest style photographs. The pamphlet represents colonial-like images of people who are presumably different from the audience who reads the pamphlet. The traffic of colonial discourse in the pamphlet evokes the assumption that the audience is curious about the exotic other while also assuming the audience's ability to be distanced from the material realities of the people in the images and those projects described within the pamphlet.

The World Bank certainly does not see itself as a colonizer; yet, as visually depicted below, there is a flexible narrative of development led by particular endowed and foreign countries in the name of fitness, orderliness, and economic productivity that shifts into a postcolonial situation.[4] The World Bank's promotional materials make clear that the countries they serve are "members" of their organization, yet, there is an embedded set of power relationships present between the "normate colonizer" (here, the World Bank) and the "backward" and "disabled" colonized (here, Third World nations), whereby the former tends to be technologically advanced and economically strong and the latter tends to have little technological advancement and a simple and vulnerable economy (Spurr 6).

In this way, the World Bank's relationship to Third World countries can be seen as a form of neocolonialism that is reified not only in the power structure present between World Bank members from First World countries but also through the image that comes from a pamphlet I collected from the resource fair at the World Bank disability conference (see figure 3.1). Unlike the Bank's policies, which focus on bringing developing countries into the global capitalism through partnerships with private

FIGURE 3.1, The cover page of the World Bank's *World Bank Group: Working for a World Free of Poverty.* World Bank, 2003.

corporate firms over supporting community-based social services, the cover to the promotional pamphlet *World Bank Group: Working for a World Free of Poverty* appears artistic and centers on the compassionate and human side of development. This pamphlet, with its colorful cover displaying "primitive" art, exhibits the Bank's goal of global development.

The top portion of the cover contains the jumble of fragmented figures, but the bottom portion appears orderly and intelligible. The words *World Bank Group*: *Working for a World Free of Poverty* mediates between the line drawings and text below it. There are hues of salmon pink, yellow, and blue below, which provide a stark contrast to the shades of green in the background image of a series of line drawings that evoke "primitive" art above. From the simple images at the top, one can detect what might represent an arm and hand, a fractured body with two feet, bent arrow ends, and layered concentric half-circles. Below the drawing, in color and in childish handwriting, is the following phrase: "The World Bank is one of the world's largest sources of funding for the developing world. Its primary focus is on helping the poorest people and the poorest countries. It uses its financial resources, its staff, and extensive experience to help developing countries reduce poverty, increase economic growth, and improve their quality of life."[5]

While the audience of this pamphlet is actually quite unclear—the conference attendees represented a vast range of people from academic researchers, NGO leaders, and private-sector companies—the pamphlet invites its readers into the process of development by guiding our eyes down the page to the colorful, logical, and concise development of *something* that makes sense, out of what is first represented as incomprehensible, archaic, disjointed, and chaotic. The juxtaposition of the fragmented and "primitive" figures with the methodical words suggests a movement toward a goal—a specific teleology, an attempt to make normal that which seems incomprehensible and incomplete. The compositional structure of this cover image represents a teleological movement away from "primitive" forms of communication (i.e., the drawings) to a more nuanced and "developed" mode (i.e., writing). The cover illustrates the act of attaining a written and comprehensible language and connotes that this form of communication is nonexistent and must be taught by a more knowledgeable group of people.

Following the common representation that people from developing nations are innocent and childlike (see Escobar), we might imagine that the above quotation was not only handwritten by a child, but a young person might also have conceived the very ideas communicated here about the Bank. For instance, the repetition of the words *poorest* and *help* and *helping*, coupled with a simple subject-verb structure, where the Bank is the central actor or subject, evokes a simplistic book report–like iteration of the organization's importance. The pamphlet's last sentence, however, contains a notable change in language that encourages the audience reading the pamphlet to safely distinguish themselves from "the other" developing nations and citizens while being empathetic without becoming directly implicated. This movement of rhetorical differentiation is facilitated by the parallel shift in the last sentence where there is an implicit discourse of development hidden within the sentence's progression. When the pamphlet states that the Bank "uses its financial resources . . . to help developing countries," it depicts the Bank as a global hero by "developing" countries (i.e., "primitive" as the visual rhetoric suggests) through the Bank's rich experience promoting development, economic, and skill viability.[6] Development and growth are two of the key means that countries—like children—might use to enhance their quality of life. At the end of the sentence, however, the objects to be saved are not individual countries. Rather, as the following phrase suggests, countries become personified actors who can "improve their quality of life."

I suggest that this attempt to personify place is rhetorically significant because the audience need not imagine that a developing country is too exotic to understand; but rather, just like the audience, the Bank's clients are working to improve this (underdeveloped) country's "quality of life." The pamphlet's text facilitates a rhetorical shift that allows audience members to differentiate themselves and yet see themselves within the Bank's primary institutional goal by contradictorily representing the people the Bank serves as both exotic other and yet "ordinary person" or perhaps even an exotic other who can become an ordinary person.

The combination of the line drawings and words also demonstrates how the Bank facilitates the teleological movement toward becoming a normal productive country that is organized, controlled, and comprehensible. Like Wolfensohn's speech above and in chapter 2, only by making what appears as "unfit fit," through teaching a standardized language, ontology, and economic practice, can Third World nations and citizens enter what Wolfensohn describes as the "mainstream" global economy ("Disability and Development"). In other words, this normalizing visual rhetoric as David Pfeifer notes, "encourages people with power and resources to label people without power and resources as abnormal" (qtd. in Davis, *Bending Over Backwards* 38). Audiences might expect that "primitive" countries or regions are not only lacking resources for "development" but also the ability (physically, socially, and culturally) to do so. The book report–like cadence of the cover's text reifies what the audience anticipates; yet, somewhat contradictorily, the whole representation simultaneously provides a tangible and visual example of "development."

The persuasiveness of this cover page depends upon the audience's estimation that Bank "clients" are primitive and thus fixed in an exotic epistemology. At the same time, however, the combination of the line drawings and words also demonstrates how the Bank facilitates the teleological movement toward becoming a productive country that is organized, controlled, and comprehensible. In this way, the audience can identify with the visual rhetoric of progression that exhibits how "developing" countries and their citizens might one day be just like the cover's audience who gazes upon them. The pamphlet's audience is invited literally to see and imagine the Bank's creation of a new global citizen who matches with the audience's own ontology. Because the validity of the Bank and its general ethos is premised upon an audience's shared cultural memory, the cover image is easily taken for granted and unquestioned.

What is striking about the above image as a whole is that the sort of intervention that the Bank imagines itself to make appears enabling or empowering (a rhetoric I explore further in chapter 4); yet, the power relationship represented here indicates that fitting into the global economy means becoming standardized and comprehensible so that the low-income country factors into the Bank's capitalist equation. As a whole, the visual rhetoric above suggests that Third World nations are unfit and even disabled; at once they reflect the teleological image categories that Garland-Thomson describes because they are "exotic," "sentimental," and eventually progress to "realistic" and comprehensible ("Politics of Staring"). The entire image reflects the common visual representation that disability is something that can be overcome and erased by proper training or by becoming coherent. The pamphlet argues that including lower-income citizens into the mainstream of development depends upon normalizing discursive frames that ignore and/or attempt to obliterate physical difference, while somewhat contradictorily arguing how the Bank intends make normal and comprehensible Third World nations and citizens.

This pamphlet traffics colonial discourses in its representation of the "primitive" and "traditional" against representations of "progress" and "development." This ideological reassembly of classic colonial discourses shows how older and seemingly forgotten ideologies actually continue to circulate and look different across multiple sites. Thus, this sort of ideological trafficking depends upon the audience's personal and cultural memory and helps to shape the dominant mode of persuasion that recurs in the pamphlet. Throughout the whole of the pamphlet, images have more rhetorical prominence than words because the *pathetic* appeals of the photos—and indeed the fact that they take up much of the pamphlet's space—invite audiences, in the words of Bhabha, to identify "ambivalently" with the pamphlet's embedded colonial narrative told through the gaze of the camera.[7] As these images show, the process of development is at once teleological and fixed, exotic and ordinary, and experienced and innocent.[8] The images, which I explore below, tend to only represent people of color and mostly in "traditional" and colorful clothing. This representation shifts the audience's attention away from the power relationships of development and toward a visual rhetoric of normalcy that secures the Bank's ethos. This visual rhetoric of care is bound up with images of the colonial other that resonate with the audience's cultural memory. However, the text of the pamphlet tells a different yet intersecting story of development. While the images function as their own narrative and allow the audience to identify with their visual effects and ignore the pamphlet's more logical description of the Bank's history, organization, and projects written alongside each photo, the very text employs (Western) surveillance.

For example, the image that is situated just below the story of Sononya Zhanazarova's, which I describe and analyze in chapter 2, pictures a middle-aged black man engaging in work. He appears to concentrate intently on turning a lever of a large machine while the camera captures his profile. The photographer behind the camera acts as an unobtrusive onlooker and frames the man's upper torso, head, and hands alongside the large machine. The audience is invited to share the photographer's gaze and simply, passively watch the man. Significantly, the man is dressed in a blue shirt with a rumpled collar. He is actively turning the lever of the machine and does not pay attention to the camera. The image suggests tenacity, industrial labor, middle-class aspirations, and productivity. In short, the audience can imagine that this man, like the other people featured in the pamphlet, is empowered by work. The visual rhetorical arguments that are produced by images like this one draw from neoliberal values of independence, work, individualism, and progress and resonate with the U.S. Personal Responsibility Act (thoroughly examined in chapter 2). At the same time, however, the images cannot be separated from the pamphlet's larger textual and visual context. The images, like the pamphlet's text, depend upon the audience's preconceived notions about people from low-income nations.

Yet, throughout the pamphlet, the textual references do not directly correspond to the visual imagery; that is, the text does not refer to the images, nor is it obvious why the image was used in that particular place. While the words in the pamphlet describe chaos and disorder alleviated by technocratic institutions that empower individuals, the visual representations depict controlled, stable, and productive people participating in limited work-related or school-related activities. The camera's gaze plays an important role in communicating familiar and identifiable values to the audience because the photographer draws on two specific modes of image making: the subject's gaze back at the camera and the camera as an unobtrusive onlooker.

Put together as an evolving narrative, all the images in the pamphlet operate at once as a forward-looking and colonial narrative. These images create knowledge about other "developing" clients or nations; yet, just as they produce new knowledge, the images examined together create a reified colonial discourse that positions citizens of the underdeveloped or developing worlds as "exotic," "idealized," and "naturalized" (Lutz and Collins 90). Bhabha, in his description of colonial discourses, likewise suggests that such discourses are dependent upon representations of fixity in the construction of otherness. This paradoxical ideological traffic—whereby rigidity and unchanging order function along with the repetition of disorder, chaos, and degeneracy—makes the World Bank's visual representations familiar and persuasive to a wide audience (66). Through this ideological traffic, the subjects in the pictures are shown wearing uniforms, sitting in rows, or in their "traditional" clothing coupled with hints of Western attire. These visual details rhetorically depict the creation of or movement toward order and compiled together the images tell their own story.

Turning to the first page of the pamphlet, the audience is confronted with a very tangible result of an improved quality of life: children playing what appears to be some version of London Bridge. The photo demonstrates children with their hands clasped together over their heads and one child moving through the human-made tunnel. The image illustrates rebirth, free time, growth, freedom, innocence, and strength (especially as a country comes out of colonialism)—thus implying for the audience what the Bank means by a high quality of life. In this way, the photo functions metonymically; the children (appearing slightly older than the child passing through the tunnel), with their collapsed hands sheltering another child, are a part of the whole result of development. The World Bank's activities assure the children's survival, their ability to stand strong, have fun, and work together with their peers. The children's Western-style clothing represents progress away from the "traditional" or "primitive" ontology offered on the pamphlet's cover and illustrates the embracement of progress and "development" (Lutz and Collins 93). To this extent, this image of children at play works against popular representations of children from low-income nations as victims of material and cultural circumstances because the children are shown playing and not suffering; yet the overarching narrative of the pamphlet's rhetoric of fitness disrupts this image.

The pamphlet's visual story begins with these children's recreational activities. Flipping through the pages of the pamphlet, however, the audience is confronted with a series of images that exemplify productivity. In every photo thereafter, the subject is doing *something* that is labor or education related—the only leisure presented is the children playing. Each photo focuses on one person, although in several of the photographs there is more than one person blurred within the camera's frame. The photos include a mixture of men, women, and children throughout the pamphlet but, significantly, all subjects are people of color.

Paging through the images, the audience is visually told the story of development. After the image of the children at play, we are confronted with a man performing fairly traditional labor: creating and folding colorful and "exotic" rugs. In this photo, the man looks only at his work and ignores the camera's gaze. The pamphlet patterns this gaze throughout; most subjects concentrate on their work and do not seem to notice the camera. For example, turning the next several pages of the pamphlet, the audience encounters a series of images that are reminiscent of photos of the colonized other. First we see a woman wearing a traditional straw hat.

FIGURE 3.2. A woman in traditional straw hat from the World Bank's *World Bank Group: Working for a World Free of Poverty*. World Bank, 2003. Tran Tai Hoa / World Bank Photo Library.

Standing in a field, she looks down at her fist full of rice or another grain. In the blurred background there are other people working to harvest the crops (see figure 3.2).

The camera appears to simply document the woman working. Nobody acknowledges the photographer. The next page shows a closeup on another person present in the background of the former photo—a man with Western-style clothing, also picking and gathering up handfuls of the plant they are harvesting. Flipping forward a couple of pages, the images, although different, continue the same pattern of representation: a man turning the lever of a machine; a female teenager, dressed in a school uniform, gathering water; girls sitting in rows studying; a woman, smiling at the sack of chilies she pours onto the ground; a female factory worker weaving material on a loom. The camera's presence is unnoticed because each subject's attention is focused on his or her work.

However, this pattern is interrupted on the fourth page, which shows a young boy facing the camera holding up a slate with the number five

FIGURE 3.3. A young boy holds a slate with the number five written on it. *World Bank Group: Working for a World Free of Poverty.* World Bank, 2003. Armi Vitale / World Bank Photo Library.

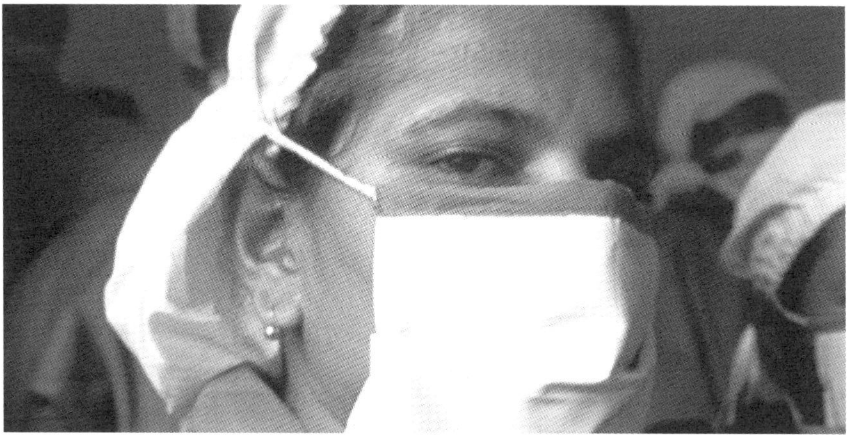

FIGURE 3.4. A woman dressed in scrubs and wearing a mask. *World Bank Group: Working for a World Free of Poverty.* World Bank, 2003. Shehzad Nooran / World Bank Photo Library.

written on it (see figure 3.3). The child has a smile on his face that illustrates pride and mastery in his work. With one eye partially covered by the slate, he looks out and directly at the camera. This act of looking, coupled with the child's expression, is significant and suggests that education gives the power to look.

Likewise, on the following page a woman, dressed in a mask and scrubs, similarly confronts the camera (see figure 3.4). These are the only photographs in the pamphlet where the subjects directly confront the camera. In this image the woman is fully clothed in Western medical attire, which suggests that the woman is highly educated. She looks over her mask directly and purposely at the camera; the audience can stare straight into her eyes. This woman's and the young boy's confrontational and direct look is powerful and significant when put into the context of the overall pamphlet and the other photographs that are included. No other subjects meet or acknowledge the camera; rather, the camera appears as an onlooker merely surveying the scene. The photographer behind the lens of the camera is not a participant in the activity shown by the image—the camera acts as reporter that oversees and demonstrates the success of development visually.

Lutz and Collins highlight the "photographer's gaze" in images such as these. Although they are examining patterns of photographs in *National*

Geographic, their observations apply here: "photographers, despite an expressed fundamental sympathy with the third world people they meet, confront them across distances of class, race, and sometimes gender. Whether from fear of differences or the more primordial (per Lacan) insecurity of the gaze itself, the photographer can often make the choice to insert technique between self and his or her subjects" (193). The photographer, based on her or his inclinations, can encourage the viewer to take interest, identify, or differentiate from the subject caught in the frame of the camera. In the observational mode, the photographer records his or her subjects unobtrusively and is detached from the photographic event. In this way, the photographer, and thus the viewer, is invited to ambivalently watch the scene and can reify the same power relationships that the image maker might seek to dispel. This form of picture taking produces a surveillance power relationship. The economy of power created through images such as these is also further complicated by the material differences between Eastern and Western countries and the position the Bank has in the "development" of a region.

The photograph of the female surgeon, who confronts the camera directly, interrupts this pattern of representation. Although one could read her act of looking as defiant, the greater context of the image suggests that the subject has entered into and embraced the colonizing gaze of the camera. The pamphlet's placement of her image in the midst of the others is significant, however. As a surgeon she wears the suitable uniform and is thus represented as controlled; yet, her education and job position reflects her "development" into a productive and intelligible global citizen. She is thus able to gaze directly into the camera and acknowledge its presence. Unlike the other subjects of the photos in the pamphlet, who have yet to attain the status of "developed," this image portrays full development. Not only is the subject working in the medical field—a field that tends to be highly respected in industrialized and postindustrialized countries—but the subject is a female. Significantly, the woman the photograph highlights is completely covered, the audience only sees her eyes—her surgical clothing covers her face, body, and hair. The audience of the pamphlet, who might assume that "underdeveloped" regions tend to have unequal gender relationships, could be moved by such an image. The woman in this image represents an evolution from a fixed ontology where women are assumed to be unequal toward gender equality. Now educated and developed, the subject has attained the power to look back. This image, along with that of the schoolboy, stands in stark contrast to the other images.

The World Bank depends upon an audience's ability to identify with the repetitive colonial othering that runs throughout all the images. Here, the World Bank's communicated goals of development are reliant upon the audience's assumption that "underdeveloped" nations are exotic, innocent, and fixed and, thus, do not fit high-income nations' economic and cultural goals. The audience, however, is able to differentiate itself from these images because the images tell a story of development that is dependent upon such separating. Thus, the pamphlet smartly tweaks this anticipated image pattern with photographs where subjects directly confront the camera. In the two representations of the doctor and the schoolboy, the audience is invited to identify not only with the subjects but also with the possibility of all the people presented in the pamphlet, because these subjects are shown as experienced (or becoming experienced), forward moving, and not unlike the audience who observes them.

In this way, these photos play an important role in this simple informative pamphlet. On their own they exhibit the Bank's ability to create a sense of order out of chaos, promote productivity over indolence, and maintain the steps toward development. This is further demonstrated in one of the final images in the pamphlet, a man fishing illustrates a key intended goal of the Bank. Again, the camera's presence is unnoticed by the subject. The subject appears to have either just caught a fish or is in the process of catching the fish. The image is powerful because it evokes the biblical parable that if one gives a man a fish he eats for a day, but if one teaches him to fish, he will eat for a lifetime.

The above examples from the World Bank pamphlet exhibit two prominent moments of ideological trafficking: metonymic stories that reflect the teleology of development and an appeal to chaos/control in development narratives. These images, together with the recurring words empower and encourage, membership, selling, market, and capital, investing, investors, and investment, and products, production, and producing (to merely name a few key clusters of terms that appear alongside the images in the pamphlet), lay out a teleological narrative that suggests that social problems might be solved by national partnerships with the private sector and microfinancing companies that are initiated by the Bank; this very teleological narrative of empowerment is explored further in chapter 4. The pamphlet appears to give Third World citizens the ability to look back and confront the Bank's audience (U.S. citizens) across a line of sight that seems to erase the power relationships between First and Third World countries. Indeed, the people the pamphlet displays ultimately appear as empowered global citizens because they reflect both neoliberal governmentality, and yet, they are still other people who come from "exotic" places.

The pamphlet's reliance on normalizing discourses through representations of tradition versus modernity shows how ideologies traffic across time. Such discourses do not have to be explained because they are ingrained within our cultural and political imaginaries, drawing upon the viewer's memory of "exotic" and "underdeveloped" places and people and colonial power relations. Even though the World Bank appears to be extending its resources to those in need, they are drawing on effective rhetorical means because they understand that ideologies traffic across time. Thus it is also important to trace the ideologies that traffic across World Bank documents because as Harlan Hahn describes, "all aspects of the environment are molded by public policy and . . . policies are a reflection of pervasive attitudes and values" (175).

The World Bank's employment of normalizing rhetorics of fitness in this pamphlet is contradictory given the problem that differently abled bodies pose for World Bank development programs. Because contemporary World Bank development programs tend to focus on making it possible for lower-income citizens to enter the labor force, people with disabilities whose nonstandard bodies cannot often engage in common laboring activities pose a conundrum for Bank policy makers. Despite the Bank's attempt to normalize people with disability into work activities, it in no way solves this conundrum; rather, the Bank perpetuates the problem by returning to deeply historic, colonial, and even eugenic discourses. For the most part, such colonial discourses traffic across this text, shoring up the text's persuasion because the legitimacy of the discourses are unquestioned and familiar. The manner in which the World Bank represents people with disabilities, as the missing links to development, is significant because the World Bank's own rhetoric is entangled in a larger ideology of able-bodied global citizenship and neoliberal economics.

As Garland-Thomson explains in her description of the contradictions of liberalism (and as I show here, neoliberalism), "the disabled figure renounc[es the] . . . very existence [of the] fiction of self-improvement and . . . present[s] the ultimate challenge to perfection and progress" (46). Likewise, this contradiction can be seen in the World Bank's embracement of neoliberalism's economics wherein the welfare state or any state dependence is seen as a sign of weakness or underdevelopment; the disabled body, then, exposes the inherent contradiction of the notion of self-reliance for citizens. Thus, people with disabilities (like all citizens) are never autonomous in the way the Bank's teleology of development promotes.[9] Supporting neoliberal economics, whereby individuals become more responsible than governments for securing their personal and community well-being, the World Bank's overarching programs and policies attempt to bring capitalism to Third World economies and in doing so lock governments and citizens into a classed system sustained by an unequal global labor market. Within capitalism, as Hahn points out, "the unemployment rate of disabled adults may be traced to broad economic forces rather than individual impairments" (173). Although according to the film *From Exclusion to Inclusion* that I examine below the World Bank seems to be trying to secure work for Third World citizens with disabilities, but for most of these people, the labor they will be able to perform will not lift them out of poverty.[10] In other words, the very global capitalist structure the World Bank promotes poses a specific problem for people with disabilities since capitalism "conceptualizes equality as equality among workers rather than financial equality" (Davis, *Bending Over Backwards* 110). How then do people with disabilities factor into this system that relies upon a standardized and able-bodied workforce?

CONTRADICTIONS: INCLUSION VS. ENABLING

The World Bank disability conference, "Disability and Inclusive Development: Sharing, Learning and Building Alliances," opened up with two short documentary films; the first was a public service announcement-style film that featured people with disabilities from across the world, and the second was a longer more traditional documentary featuring the filmmaker himself and interviews with people. The films were meant to be celebratory in the sense that the conference was seeking to be inclusive and positive about disability in general. The film *From Exclusion to Inclusion*, for example, demonstrated the way that the World Bank is working to factor people with disabilities into the administrative structures at the World Bank itself and into development projects at large. Like the above analyzed pamphlet, this film employs a similar neoliberal rhetoric of fitness that emphasizes work, personal tenacity, and cultural homogenization. Yet, the film takes the rhetoric of fitness a step further to suggest that becoming fit means overcoming and, at times, literally erasing difference and disability. In doing so, the film constructs disability and accommodation as the responsibility of the individual who should not "cause undue hardship" for those without disabilities (Jung 130). In other words, the film suggests, not unlike the post-Beijing gender mainstreaming policies I look at in chapter 2 and then the empowerment rhetorics I explore in chapter 4, that if one has enough tenacity and can make accommodations for one's disability, then one will fit into a global economy. The film ultimately reinforces the belief "that accommodation is the responsibility of the one who does not fit" (Jung 131).

The film begins by reminding the audience that there are six hundred million people around the world that have one or more kinds of disabilities and then transitions to individual frames of several people in succession talking about their own disabilities. This portion of film is not in color, but in muted tones of brown. Each person sits against a dark background and is dressed in professional clothing, and most speak English or American Sign Language (ASL). Because the camera frames their upper torsos, we do not "see" or get a sense of the subjects' disability—and it appears that, in fact, the disability has been overcome, erased.[11] Looking directly into the camera and speaking about their own experiences, this set of articulate people illustrates the Bank's definition of inclusion and development. The brown tones coupled with the camera's focus and the uniformly dressed speakers represent the standard working body. At this point in the film, the camera's gaze works against the common representation of "the disabled victim" and rhetorically does not evoke feelings of "antipathy and aversion" in the film's audience (Hahn 176). Instead, the audience identifies with the articulate and controlled individuals in front of us.

As the film continues however, the audience is introduced to the World Bank's global disability and development programs; we learn what the World Bank is doing to "include" people with disabilities who live in the Third World. Yet, we do not hear directly from the people participating in the World Bank's programs—instead, we see them in action. In contrast to the professionally dressed subjects of the first scene who speak directly to the camera, look able-bodied, and appear in monotone color, the nonadministrative participants in the World Bank's disability program are filmed in full color and do not look at or speak to the camera; rather we observe them unobtrusively. The camera renders their actions awkward and in doing so begs for the audience's empathy; the camera focuses closely on them shuffling on crutches while planting a garden, wheeling in a wheelchair around a mushroom-growing warehouse, and using differently functioning arms and hands to create various commodities.

The camera's upward angle leads the audience to stare at and focus on the Third World subject's disfigurement, rendering the body into a working object "to-be-looked-at and not-to-be-looked at" (Garland-Thomson, "Politics of Staring" 57). In each instance the subjects in the camera's inconspicuous gaze engage in work-related activities—indeed, in each instance there is also slippage between the enabled fit global subject-citizen-worker and the freakish and backward Third World underdeveloped object. The camera angles and panned out frames lead the audience to categorize each individual as a nonnormative or substandard body in contrast to those people at the beginning of the film that appear controlled, standard, and "normal."

The visual rhetoric suggests that the person with the disability disrupts the work environment, not that the work environment needs to be enabling. *From Exclusion to Inclusion* tells a teleological story of development, it suggests that those who have become part of development have become standardized working bodies and enabled subjects whose voices count, who can tell their history, who have, ultimately, overcome their disability. In other words, the group of people the film begins with stand in stark contrast to the Third World people with visible disabilities the Bank is working both to "include" and make fit.

Just after this film, and without a break or discussion, the conference showed Pineda's film (he was also present in the audience). Importantly, while both films employ rhetorics of fitness in this same occasion, each film has vastly different messages. These films shown one after the other at the same occasion and using the same terms demonstrate the ideological traffic of fitness. In other words, the same occasion, time, even place does not necessarily determine same rhetorical meaning. Accordingly, it is important for rhetoricians to trace and analyze rhetorics across a single occasion. Moreover, unlike the colonial discourses trafficking in the earlier discussion of the World Bank materials and following Alexander's recognition, different histories (in this case, activist histories, histories of the gaze, common representations of disability) are the ideologies trafficking in these films. As a result, it is important to understand that disability activists (especially radical ones) have historically worked to disrupt notions of normalcy. Drawing on queer notions of embodiment, where bodies are not made to fit standard categorizations of sex, gender, or sexuality, disability activists seek to open up how the able-bodied relate to their world, showing how a disability perspective can help create new physical environments, ways of thinking, and ways of doing. Thus, Pineda's film is important because it demonstrates a shift in ideological traffic, drawing attention to the limits of a narrow version of neoliberal development, making people across the globe personally responsible for normalizing citizens into formal laboring activities.

In the film, then, Pineda offers a different rhetoric of fitness and in doing so exposes the problems of neoliberal universal work programs that emphasize personal responsibility, tenacity, and homogeneity, because he shows how people with disabilities tend to be underpaid and marginalized and also how differently functioning bodies themselves disrupt work environments. Even though I do believe that Pineda's *A World Enabled* importantly redefines fitness, I do not want to blindly celebrate it. There are times when the film falls into individualist narratives of experience, and in doing so it often disconnects the people Pineda meets and the locations Pineda travels to from their complex and wider contexts. For example, he does not address how socialist Yugoslavia was replaced by structural adjustment or how the role of the United Nations, World Bank, IMF, United States, and NATO helped to shape the ethnic and religious conflicts there and in the Balkans at large. These personal narratives often reify teleological narratives of development and tend to also focus on individual bodies. Nevertheless, unlike the film *From Exclusion to Inclusion*, where bodies are only shown working and disconnected from the politics of work, Pineda does demonstrate how individual bodies expose the contradictions and resist economic neoliberalism and neoliberal governmentality by connecting those bodies to their environments.

In the film, Pineda visits the war-torn Balkans, socialist Cuba, and progressive Berkeley, California. As he visits these regions and countries the audience sees him navigate with his wheelchair a variety of terrains. In doing so, he demonstrates the way in which the environment can be enabling or disabling for a person with disabilities, if not all people. Pineda shifts the ideological traffic around disability away from its colonialist and normalizing discourse by reframing the very notion of fitness; fitness is not tied to an individual body but rather to the body politic and, moreover, the global body politic. In other words, unlike the unidirectional argument where ultimately development means individuals engaging in coherent work activities and nations organizing their economies to fit with wealthy nations, the film exposes how these sorts of development plans are, in the end, shortsighted and harmful for those from lower-income nations. In short, Pineda exposes how the disabled body will never be standard and in doing so illustrates the need for universal design. Like the Beijing Platform I examine in chapter 2, Pineda networks his argument for universal design to some (although not all) of the wider social and economic systems that would help make the environment fit for a variety of people. By making these connections, *A World Enabled* recasts the definition of fitness away from the individual body (and individual actions) to infrastructures that can promote an environment fit for all.

The first place Pineda visits in the film is Serbia. In this portion of the film he connects disability to wider contexts like war and social stigma. He makes it clear that fitness is never possible in war, quite literally no body may be working (formally), and therefore, it is impossible to focus on individual tenacity. As the film begins, we hear Pineda as he describes the situation in the Balkans: "The people in Yugoslavia have endured civil wars, NATO bombings, and political isolation. These processes have continued to disable its people" (*A World Enabled*). This statement is spoken over violent images of war and the sound of Croatian, Bosnian, or Serbian rap music, the English-speaking listener can detect the words "Coca-Cola" and "business men." Although I do not speak any of these languages, I read the inclusion of this song with the statement Pineda makes about what has happened to Yugoslavia as a critique of how capitalism has not solved the ethnic tensions in this area of the world and then how those tensions have hindered and disabled many members of the area's population. Pineda's opening begins to rhetorically shift the notion of fitness away from changing a person to instead recognizing how *all* people become disabled by war and that *all* people benefit from wider infrastructural support. Many of the images from this portion of the film show Pineda attempting to navigate broken terrains with his wheelchair—many of which result in somebody carrying him in his chair down narrow and crumbling stairs.

This imagery of Pineda trying to move his wheelchair over rough surfaces continues in the part of the film that depicts his visit to Cuba. The scene begins with the following phrase: "Cuba is at once a paradox between the simple joys of life and the complex forces that restrain it. The last bastion of Communism survives on this tropical island. It suffers from an unrelenting embargo, and stifled foreign trade. Everyday becomes an attempt to cope with the consequences of an isolated ideology" (*A World Enabled*). Over festive Cuban music and images of Cuba's geography he explains: "I had come to Cuba to see how disabled people lived, but most of all I wanted to *experience* this different reality" (*A World Enabled*; emphasis added). After this phrase we see images of people walking over various terrains interspersed with a few images of people being pushed in wheelchairs or using crutches. This brief scene ends by showing a man working on navigating a curb with his wheelchair; he ends up sitting on the ground, lifting the chair up, and then gets back in. Pineda then explains further, "I had come to Cuba to see how disabled people lived, to see how social and economic conditions could further or limit [people]. I wanted to explore the system of services and support" (*A World Enabled*). What Pineda then goes on to explain is how the U.S. embargo has directly impacted people with disabilities because, due to the embargo, "basic equipment is not available" (*A World Enabled*). Nonetheless, through interviews with a variety of people, Pineda comes to the conclusion that Cubans are living through the worst and best period in history. Due to the U.S. embargo and lack of Soviet trade Cubans do not have access to materials that support their universal health care and educational system; yet the availability of these systems make it a good time for Cubans.

However, what Pineda notices about the island is that there are few people with disabilities around. He finds them in rehabilitation centers and labor institutions that he critiques as sequestering and separating people with disabilities. As he makes clear, this sort of "mainstreaming" into formal work activities can be isolating and, as a result, make it possible for the government (and citizens) to ignore the environmental and cultural needs of people with disabilities because they are literally invisible. During a visit to one of the factories that employs people with disabilities he learns that the workers are only paid five cents per case of razors they assemble and that there were 175 razors per case. Pineda himself helps assemble razors, and the audience sees how complicated the process of folding and packing the razors can be, especially for a person with a disability. This scene then, begins to demonstrate the confines of putting people with disabilities to work by drawing attention to the restrictions that some bodies have and thus the limitations of development programs that emphasize personal responsibility and work over social and cultural development programs that would create infrastructures not just for people with disabilities but all people.

Just after this scene, the camera shifts to a luxurious spa-like hospital. Pineda explains how, because Cuba has a surplus of highly skilled doctors and a shortfall of supplies, the country has tried to bring money in through developing health tourism. Yet, these services are not available to most Cubans and, due to the U.S. embargo, this sort of development program has ended up not bringing much money to the island. Pineda explains, "In many ways [Cuba's] education and health care advancements are great achievements. For example universal health coverage and a literacy rate of over 97 percent are not even present in most developed countries. Although Cuba does provide universal health care and education as a human right, free of charge, it does so [for people with disabilities] in confined environments" (*A World Enabled*). Much like the Beijing Platform analyzed in chapter 2, Pineda networks the needs of people with disabilities not simply to basic neoliberal economic development (which merely emphasizes standardizing people and putting them to work regardless of their physical and mental abilities) but rather he shows how successful development programs must focus on infrastructures such as health care and education. However, Pineda not only disrupts the World Bank's overarching narrative that development means becoming coherent but also exposes and interrupts the World Bank's rhetoric of fitness. He shifts the ideological traffic by drawing attention to how confined work environments, which we see in both films—in *From Exclusion to Inclusion* the mushroom-growing facility was only staffed by people with disabilities, and in *A World Enabled* we see people with disabilities assembling and packing razors—hide people with disabilities and in doing so unwittingly emphasize that disabilities are shameful and thus hidden. This hiding however, makes it easy for a nation to not develop infrastructures such as wheelchair ramps, accessible public transportation, and other forms of adaptive technologies or universal designs. Pineda further networks his arguments beyond economic development and ends the scene in Cuba with the following reflection: "My sense of freedom and personal independence was sequestered on this island by insurmountable physical living conditions and inadequate nutrition. . . . In fact I needed twenty-four hour care and assistance. The loss of physical freedom proved to be my biggest obstacle and led to the contemplation of my disability and my freedom in a whole new light" (*A World Enabled*).

As Pineda demonstrates, until people with disabilities have more basic needs covered, such as mobility and visibility, they will not be a part of their community (let alone global community) or even be recognized as vital and contributing part of their communities, especially because they will only be seen as needing help. Moreover, merely putting a disabled body to work, without addressing the physical environment and long-held belief systems about personal autonomy and disability, ultimately ends up remarginalizing people with disabilities. Pineda recognizes that visibility (literally being a person on the street with a disability) and physical mobility are the first steps in giving a person with a disability agency. Without that agency, then, a person with a disability cannot fit into the World Bank normalizing narrative of global development as becoming a coherent, industrious, and independent worker because his or her ontology will never be coherent.

In the final scene of the short film, Pineda visits Berkeley, California. The scene opens up with Pineda reading the following quotation: "We have said for two hundred years that we do not wish to see disabled people. We do not want to be reminded of their needs, or burdened with their desire to live in the world and we prefer these people to be sequestered safely in secluded institutions, and they have been. We prefer them to be invisible, and they strive, many of them, to be so, in hopes of perhaps that way finally of gaining our acceptance" (Bowe qtd. in *A World Enabled*). Pineda goes on to link the United States' disability activist movement to other civil rights movements throughout the 1960s and 1970s. Centering on Berkeley, California, and using images from the disability rights movement, the film suggests that the protests drew attention to how the physical environment of Berkeley made it impossible for people with disabilities to get around the city independently. As Pineda makes clear, the disability activists sought to change "the rules of living with a disability"; the protesters showed that they "did not want to be seen as helpless medical patients" (*A World Enabled*). Instead, the activists fought for "full inclusion of the disability community in social participation through active involvement in policy and planning. Here people with disabilities created their own plan for inclusion by changing the built physical environment, demanding accessible transportation, and sensitizing public understanding" (*A World Enabled*). After recounting Berkeley's history with the disability rights movement, the film goes on to interview four people with disabilities of different sorts, each who explain how because of Berkeley's accessible environment and stigma-free culture, they are successful in their careers as students, city planners, therapists, and computer programmers; crucially, none of the interviewees suggest that it was due to their personal tenacity or due to their family that they have been able to be part of the community. As one of the interviewees, a student at Berkeley, explains, "Social factors influence quality of life more than the degree to which somebody is physically impaired" (*A World Enabled*). Just after this young woman's statement Pineda adds, "The disability rights movement addresses . . . [the] elimination of physical barriers, [and] it attacks the social barriers that continue to disable those with impairments. Berkeley offers city planners, policy makers, and the world a unique model of inclusion" (*A World Enabled*). The film, particularly in its focus on Berkeley and its emphasis on social factors, physical barriers, and infrastructure, networks its arguments for disability and development programs to a wide variety of quality of life factors that not only influence a person with disabilities' ability to work but also the ability for everybody to participate (make decisions, have a voice, and be seen) in public life. However, a downfall of the film, and perhaps showing how neoliberal governmentality imbues all our lives, Pineda does not recognize the economic wealth that a place like

Berkeley can offer or how these individualizing narratives reinforce notions of self-sufficiency.

Nevertheless, showing these two films at a single occasion offered a conjunctural moment whereby the limitations and contradictions of the World Bank's overarching rhetoric of fitness, through the trafficking of normalizing and standardization ideologies, became clear. Pineda's film offered a glaring critique of neoliberalism and at the same time demonstrated the colonialist and normalizing discourses that traffic throughout the World Bank's development plans. At the very least, Pineda's physical limitations showed the necessity of public services and public infrastructures, many of which, as I describe in chapters 1 and 2, were part of the feminist conception of gender mainstreaming but then disappeared as supranational organization and policies made lower-income nations cut these sorts of programs. Conjunctural moments may appear as occasional, immediate, or even accidental, but it is a moment when "the previously existing disposition of social forces" shift (Gramsci 178). I suggest because of this occasion, this ultimate conjunctural moment, new activist rhetorics of fitness emerged to further critique neoliberal and normalizing discourses as they relate to globalization.

While we cannot trace the exact instances when this conjunctural moment resulted in a counter-hegemonic discourse, the World Bank's subsequent disability and development initiatives show an interesting convergence of the two contradictory rhetorics of fitness. Although I believe that the disability conference was supposed to be an annual or biannual event, to my knowledge, the World Bank has not hosted a conference since then. In looking at their various reports, publications, and website, it is clear that instead of taking the lead on disability and development initiatives, the World Bank has relied upon other organizations and disability activists themselves to plan and carry out projects for people with disabilities.

CONJUNCTURAL MOMENTS AND A REVISED RHETORIC OF FITNESS

By tracing the ideological traffic we can see how rhetorics connect to each other, how arguments are networked to the past and then are reiterated in the present. Neoliberal arguments attempt to eschew the past and invent the new (i.e., the "neo" part in neoliberal) so that arguments become detached from their contexts and histories. In this chapter, then, I work to network arguments to those histories and contexts to show how ideologies from the past traffic in texts of the present. Following the transnational feminist Alexander, this chapter reminds us that we have to draw back to this history so that we can see how power always has history and in order to trace the pretexts that inform on the ground policies and development initiatives. While this chapter demonstrates how to perform a transnational feminist rhetorical analysis on a single occasion, by making note of how historical ideologies traffic across various texts and often remarginalize particular groups of people, I also offer briefly how single occasions can lead to a conjunctural moment of possibility—moments where it becomes clear that arguments must become networked to wider contexts. These moments can produce what I explore further in chapter 4 and what J. K. Gibson-Graham describe as interarticulations.

After the World Bank conference on disability in 2004, the World Bank's website began to (literally) link to other disability and development organizations and concerns. In so doing, the World Bank networked its arguments for inclusive disability policies to wider contexts, much like the Beijing Platform does. However, the Bank also noted how social stigmas about disability relate to these wider contexts, including the need for adaptive technologies and universal design. Moving away from a unidirectional rhetoric of fitness that means teaching people with disabilities to work, they began to note how this process was not so easy because of the deeply historical stigma many cultures and communities have about people with disabilities. The World Bank references the Millennium Development goals, thereby recognizing the need for people with disabilities to be involved in their communities—especially through assistive technologies; it describes the following goal:

> The main goal is divided into three steps: increasing awareness, reducing preventable disabilities, and most important, integrating persons with disabilities into the social and economic life of their communities. Disability needs to be placed as an issue along others on the development agenda, and programs aimed at decreasing malnutrition, promoting maternal health, and promoting safe living and working conditions must be developed. However, even with widespread prevention programs there will always be persons with disabilities in the world, starting with the substantial disabled population that

> already exists. Efforts of inclusion are needed to remove all barriers preventing persons with disabilities from full participation in all areas of a community. In the end no distinction should be made between a disabled person's and non-disabled person's freedom to participate in every facet of life—social, economic, and political. ("Disability—Frequently Asked Questions")

I quote, at length, how the Millennium Development goals address disability because in this brief statement we can see the results of the conjunctural moment at the Bank conference in 2004. Moving away from the World Bank's common neoliberal rhetoric of fitness, this statement connects disability with ability by integrating people with disabilities into the social *and* economic lives of their community while also redefining the term "inclusion" to mean not inclusion only into economic structures but *removing* the barriers (physical and stigma) that prevent people with disabilities from being active in their communities. This statement moves away from rhetorics of fitness that emphasize individual people and extends fitness to mean fit communities. It also networks a person with a disability's well-being to poverty, malnutrition, and maternal health—the very same concerns that people without disabilities also have and also the very same concerns of the Beijing Platform. The statement ends, much like the film *A World Enabled*, by drawing attention to the notion of making the environment fit for people with disabilities, specifically noting that people with disabilities ought to be able enjoy the same sorts of freedoms that people without disability strive for.

Crucially, while the above statement might be read as the World Bank ignoring or erasing differences between people with and without a disability, the following statement demonstrates how its rhetoric of fitness has shifted as it recognizes multiple ways of living and being and multiple ways that people define themselves: "The World Bank supports disabled people developing their own language, and recommends asking individuals with disabilities for his/her preference. . . . Some prefer the term 'persons with disabilities' to emphasize the person first and the disability as secondary, while others promote the term 'disabled people' to emphasize the role society has in their disability" ("Disability—Frequently Asked Questions"). In this statement, we can see disability activists' ideological traffic. As I mention above, disability rights activists have fought to make their communities more physically inclusive and have also worked to define their own needs and desires. This statement reflects the film *A World Enabled* as it makes direct reference to agency as supported by infrastructures while also recognizing how development initiatives must include the grassroots whereby diverse communities of people articulate their diverse needs. In other words, in this instance we also see how rhetorics of fitness are transcoded and redefined to situate the individual within social and environmental structures.

Tracking networked arguments in a single occasion allows us to see conjunctural moments—a moment of possibility—as the revised rhetoric of fitness employed by the World Bank demonstrates. As I show in the next chapter, transnational feminist rhetoricians must network arguments to work against ideological traffic by shifting rhetoric in positive ways. Unlike the beginning of this chapter and prior chapters in which I read policies for their dominant power structures, the next chapter picks up on these moments of possibility and shows how a transnational feminist rhetorical analytic moves away from only critiquing globalization's effects and toward noticing its unevenness, variability, and promise.

4 EMPOWERMENT

The following discussion was reproduced in a *Wall Street Journal* article published just after the International Conference on Population and Development in Cairo, Egypt, in 1994—the third decennial conference to address issues of population growth, fertility, and development particularly in the so-called Second and Third Worlds:

> "We have no term for 'female empowerment,'" apologizes a woman who does French translations for the UN. . . .
>
> "Who is empowering whom?" asks a bewildered Chinese translator. "We can't work it out," he says. . . .
>
> "'Female empowerment' is such a vague terminology that I doubt it exists in any language but English," says Mika Kusmenko, the UN's Russian translation chief. "Our translation of it doesn't mean much, either, so I guess it's accurate." (Waldman)

The article goes on to talk about the ways in which the Cairo Programme of Action, a guiding document for international population policy, is fraught with "linguistic chaos" (Cairo Programme of Action 2). For not only did the rhetoric of "women's empowerment" frame the UN Conference on Population and Development and its final Programme of Action, the terms and concepts that supported this rhetoric, such as *family planning* and *family leave* or *maternity leave*, do not easily translate across borders either. As the discussion above demonstrates, the rhetoric of global women's empowerment is neither simple nor particularly clear.

While certainly (and as I show further below) the argument for women's empowerment has its roots in second- and third-wave feminist consciousness raising, the concept as it appears in late twentieth-century global policy circles is what Saul Halfon describes as a "rather open-ended, free-floating, signifier" (83) that could stand for women's access to health care, political action, personal agency, the right to speak, the ability to work outside the home, the right to maintain cultural practices, or often some combination of all these. And certainly, as the *Wall Street Journal* suggests, the term loses its stability of meaning as it is translated across nation-state borders.

Interestingly, the Population and Development Conference of 1994, and its rhetoric of women's empowerment, was remarkably different from past Population and Development conferences. The 1994 conference, for example, included the voices not only of demographers and economists, who in the past focused on the relationship between fertility and economic growth, but also those of feminist academics and NGO leaders who contributed knowledge about the wide variety of factors that influence a woman's ability to control her fertility and individual families' ability to reduce infant and maternal mortality. Crucially, the 1994 conference finalized the Cairo Programme of Action, which advances a new philosophy about population policy—one that downplays a traditional demographic focus on population level statistics, which simply connect the number of children a woman has with her economic well-being. Unlike past international population documents, the Cairo Programme centers on the relationship between individual women's health and their reproductive choices, on women's access to education prospects and job possibilities, and on women having a political voice as part of a larger rhetoric of "women's empowerment." Moreover, by radically linking, for example, the concept of empowerment to "the elimination of all forms of violence against women [and] ensuring women's ability to control their own fertility," the Cairo Programme demonstrates how these two seemingly disparate issues are "cornerstones of population and development-related" policies (7) and thus shows how women's empowerment depends deeply upon cultural, economic, and structural changes, not simply women's personal decisions.

During the preconvention discussions that helped to construct the Cairo Programme, feminists (from both wealthy and poor nations) in particular made it clear that for population and development policies to support women's reproductive choices those policies must focus on sustainable economic development, not individual women's reproductive choices. Feminists argued that the Cairo Programme needed to expand beyond a focus on just reproduction and population growth. Like the feminists argued at Beijing, the Cairo Programme must include larger *contextual* issues that relate to women's empowerment such as their overall access to general health services, the imbalance between women's and men's domestic responsibilities, environmental degradation, *and* how each of these has been affected by structural adjustment policies,[1] development loans, community norms, as well as local, ethnic, cultural, and familial practices (see McIntosh and Finkle).

In other words, although the Cairo Programme does not directly define *women's empowerment* (and certainly the *Wall Street Journal* report suggests that the indeterminate phrase is not easily translated), the final Programme clearly links the topos *empowerment* to arguments for "sustained economic growth in the context of sustainable development," "education . . . for girls," "gender equity and equality," and "universal access to reproductive health services, including family planning and sexual health" (Cairo Programme of Action 6). Ultimately, the Cairo Programme contends that women's empowerment is intrinsically linked to wider contextual issues that affect a woman's ability to make decisions about her life, her body, her family, and her community. The Cairo Programme certainly influenced the Beijing Platform's networked arguments for gender mainstreaming that I explore in chapter 2.

Although international conferences and their resulting statements of action only offer the global community nonbinding resolutions and recommendations, they do set the tone for what constitutes internationally accepted policy practices. Consequently, documents such as the Cairo Programme can exert pressure on the global community to conform to their recommendations; the way in which the rhetoric of women's empowerment—even in the Beijing Platform, for example—began to circulate globally within subsequent, post-Cairo gender policies is a good example. Perhaps due to the feminist notion that women's empowerment is not simply about women's individual choices but about how personal agency is affected by wider environmental, cultural, political, and economic issues (as also reflected by the disability activists' work I explore at the end of chapter 3), after the Cairo conference, the phrases *women's empowerment* and *the empowerment of women* did gain a certain pro-woman cachet. Even though the *Wall Street Journal* suggests that the term *empowerment* does not easily translate across nation-state borders, the phrase *women's empowerment* in fact has been readily employed in several local and global policies.[2] However, whereas we can ascertain the grassroots rhetoric of women's empowerment in the drafts of the Cairo Programme, several subsequent renditions of this rhetoric have been used to frame policies that regulate women's bodies, to isolate individual needs from community needs, and to affectively link individuals from wealthy nations to women from poorer nations.

Like the preceding chapters, which trace how transnational networks enable commonplace arguments in policies, development plans, and guiding documents to be easily assimilated within a neoliberal policy structure, in this chapter, I demonstrate how policy makers and global institutions have reframed the feminist term *empowerment* to legislate neoliberal practices that actually reinstitute the very structures that limited women's empowerment in the first place. Unlike the other chapters, however, in which I read policies for their dominant (and dominating) power structures, in this chapter I also employ an analytic of *interarticulation* to examine how empowerment rhetorics function variably while they maintain a seemingly static definition. Thus, the way in which global and local institutions employ the phrase *women's empowerment* should be of crucial concern for feminist rhetoricians because, although its rhetoric can suggest a positive and pro-woman agenda, the phrase is often deployed to legislate practices that in fact are not empowering and that may further disenfranchise women. Like the neoliberal rhetorics I explore throughout this book, post Cairo the phrase *women's empowerment*, for example, tends to connect empowerment merely with personal decisions or agency, delinking wider cultural, gendered, economic, and political contexts from its meaning. Tracing the rhetoric of women's empowerment as it circulates in global policy networks reveals how, as presumed commonplace arguments circulate across borders, their meanings can change.

While the term *empowerment* has certainly been used throughout the last few decades of feminist organizing within the United States and elsewhere, it generally has supported a pro-woman agenda whereby women experience empowerment when political and social structures are in place to support them on a personal level *and* a community level. Starting in the 1970s, for example, the Boston Women's Health Coalition (who compiled the well-known *Our Bodies, Ourselves* series) described women's knowledge of their bodies, being able to care for them, and access to quality health care as a form of empowerment. Likewise, liberal U.S. feminists throughout the 1970s and 1980s connected women's empowerment to their access to political office. Then, in the 1980s and 1990s, U.S. social workers also embraced the notion that empowering poor women through education and consciousness raising might lift them out of poverty. In these examples, empowerment does not come from above but rather through collective community organizing alongside self-determination. Indeed, in her groundbreaking book *Black Feminist Thought: Knowledge, Consciousness, and the Politics of Empowerment*, Patricia Hill Collins equates empowerment with social justice, education, and community *as well as* self-definition and self-reliance. Although for Collins, empowerment must come from within, it is enabled by a wider support system (119). Empowerment is not merely personal but made possible by a complex matrix of situations; according to Collins, because oppressions are linked, they therefore necessitate "transforming unjust social institutions" (273). Perhaps drawing from feminist scholars like Collins (and as I address further below), in the 1990s the Gender and Development (or GAD) movement also embraced a rhetoric of women's empowerment that worked against other development paradigms. For example, the GAD approach challenged in-kind global welfare development models of the 1980s, which emphasized a top-down approach to poverty alleviation, and instead embraced a bottom-up model whereby women themselves defined their personal and community needs. The Cairo Programme reflects the GAD approach by advocating not only a feminist definition but also a feminist *practice* of empowerment.

However, in direct contradiction to empowerment rhetorics' feminist genealogy, post Cairo several subsequent gender policies merely define women's empowerment as a woman's ability to make economic choices to thrive in and support a growing transnational capitalist economy. Like rhetorics of mainstreaming and fitness, then, neoliberal empowerment models tend to focus solely on individual economic advancement and tend to follow a therapeutic and emotional political project that places emphasis on personal decisions and affective connections over a feminist definition of women's empowerment that considers how broader contexts influence individual women.

Neoliberal global gender policies often embrace a model of empowerment that is not feminist and that supports the notion that empowerment is bequeathed onto one from another; in this version of empowerment, the granter can easily take power away (Rowlands 12). Accordingly, as Jo Rowlands aptly notes in her description of how empowerment is used in global gender policies post Cairo: "Women's empowerment, is . . . an instrumentalist approach to achieving the economic growth of the developmentalist discourse, where the placing of emphasis on women becomes a means to a particular end" (13). As women are "empowered" by a Westernized consciousness—and thus brought into "development" (or one might even say their consciousness is "colonized")—they become "empowered" to participate in dominant economic and political structures that often do not reflect their own community or individual needs and desires and that often reinforce the very structures that subjugate them (Rowlands 12). Consequently, as policy makers, NGOs, and governments move from the twentieth century into the twenty-first century, the rhetoric of women's empowerment in their policies ends up being even more vague and complex than what the *Wall Street Journal* originally suggested in the mid-1990s.

Interarticulation highlights the ways in which a network of relationships impact rhetorics' transnational circulation. As Inderpal Grewal explains, we must pay attention to how the local is structured by the global, how the local is always connected to the global through the movement of goods, people, and ideas across nation-state boundaries (28). In this way, Grewal draws attention to the importance of looking at transnational rhetorical acts outside of a static rhetorical situation. As I explore in chapter 1, recent rhetorical scholars have critiqued the closed rhetorical situation of speaker, text, and audience, while also considering how rhetorical exigencies and external contexts shape a rhetorical act and how rhetorics are always in motion. I suggest that as policy rhetorics travel, they gather a palimpsest of contexts and a nexus of interarticulations that affect meaning.

As I also discussed in chapter 1 of this book, because public policy does not have a discrete writer or actor, to understand the rhetoric of public policy, critics must account for how policy networks and shifting contexts inform an isolated rhetorical act and thus affect our reception and understanding of it. While we can read public policy for its themes and ideographs, to understand a common rhetorical phrase's overarching argument, we must examine that specific rhetorical act in relation to other rhetorical acts and within varying contexts in order to show its instability of meaning.

Following J. K. Gibson-Graham and Grewal, then, I suggest *interarticulation* as a rhetorical concept that can help us account for both the shifting meanings and unevenness of rhetorics as they travel in international policies. Interarticulation addresses how, for example, although policy arguments for women's empowerment appear monolithic, as the arguments circulate transnationally, they become composed of elements derived from different things that are distinctly joined or marked. In other words, by examining the various interarticulations of empowerment across policies, development plans, guiding documents, and even global charity campaigns, feminist rhetoricians can begin to trace first how the term *empowerment* is not stable and second how the term is used to justify policy plans that might, in fact, *dis*empower women.

Moreover, Gibson-Graham recognizes that because "the [transnational] economic landscape is . . . populated by a myriad of contingent forms and interarticulations [it is necessary to employ] the technique of reading for difference rather than [just] dominance" (54). Unlike transnational feminist scholars such as Gibson-Graham, Grewal, and Chandra Mohanty, scholars of classic globalization such as Immanuel Wallerstein, Etienne Balibar, and Liah Greenfeld tend to focus on the local without a cogent analysis of how the local is embedded within scales of globalization. These sorts of studies (and indeed some feminist rhetorical scholars as well)[3] then often examine how global economic, cultural, and discursive practices only reify hierarchal structures such as the dominance of the First World over the Third World—in fact, some of my earlier work and chapters have, to some extent, made this assumption as well. Yet, this assumption can be misleading. More recent scholarship in globalization and transnational studies have tended to emphasize flows, circulations, and networks and seek to study how the local or micro is always already linked to the macro or global (see Arjun Appadurai, Michael Hardt and Antonio Negri, Aiwa Ong, Anthony Giddens, Auturo Escobar, and Saskia Sassen). Such scholars also tend to note that we need to think about relationships within scales and in doing so recognize how power is not just about how one locale dominates another.

Thus, crucial to the development of a transnational feminist rhetorical analysis, Gibson-Graham also highlights the concept of interarticulation in order to move feminist scholars away from merely critiquing the workings of globalization and toward recognizing the wide-range effects of globalization; they do this because, ultimately, binary logics limit our understanding of complex global realities. Accordingly, a transnational feminist rhetorical analytic must trace how contexts *and* interarticulations impact a rhetoric's meaning so that feminist rhetoricians can understand the *diverse* material effects of globalization—including positive material effects. When scholars only look to critique, they may miss the relational or emancipating possibilities of rhetoric.

Empowerment, the rhetoric that frames this chapter, may, for example, look similar across a variety of texts, but ultimately the commonplace term might frame different arguments, carry different meanings, and have distinct material effects depending on context and location—especially as we follow this rhetoric through the so-called First and Third Worlds (McRuer 11). In some policies, the term *empowerment* functions productively (and therefore reflects feminist intentions); at other times, the term *empowerment* operates restrictively. The logic of interarticulation will demonstrate how such a term can circulate effectively within both feminist discourse and within a neoliberal capitalist framework.

My central argument of this chapter, then, is twofold. My first claim is that neoliberal policies that include the term *empowerment* or the phrase *women's empowerment* can appear benign because the rhetoric of empowerment seemingly strengthens policy makers' pro-woman ethos due to the term's feminist history. This misappropriation thus allows a wide audience to ignore the policy's actual material practices—whether those practices are positive for women or not. To illustrate this inconsistency, I examine the history of empowerment rhetorics within the development community along with a diverse set of global women's empowerment policies and programs ranging from UNIFEM programs of actions and UN documents to the World Bank women's development policies and mircolending plans. These examples demonstrate the sorts of interarticulated arguments that circulate globally at the end of the twentieth century and offer illustrations of their differing representational and programmatic impact. Like my earlier chapters, in this chapter I show how the arguments I trace sometimes reflect late twentieth-century neoliberal economics and ideologies and thus draw from common (and historically embedded) representations of the poor, focusing on the individual as an agent for economic change and attempting to make standard particular gendered ways of acting.

My second claim is that as the term *empowerment* is interarticulated within other development policy contexts, the term's meaning continues to shift. The term *empowerment* may account for how women's well-being is determined by a wide variety of factors, including personal and community agency, political voice, and women's ability to shape the policies that affect their families and community, as it does in the Cairo Programme of Action. And yet, still in other renditions, empowerment becomes an affective neoliberal term that mircolending institutions use to describe not only the results of their programs (i.e., lending empowers women from poorer nations) but also to describe the lender's feelings (i.e., the lender feels empowered by lending money). The empowerment rhetoric of microlending further supports a neoliberal agenda through its focus on the individual and on colonial stereotypes, but the rhetoric also affectively animates individual lenders, situating them as activist neoliberal subjects by shifting attention away from individual poor women and onto the personal emotional power of empowerment. Thus, empowerment—the practice and the feeling—is an affective networking tool that serves as a way to link individuals across nations. In this way, microlending is not just a way to move money from one location to another, but it also enables a symbiotic exchange of feeling whereby the lower-income citizen, by simply being available to accept the loan, "empowers" the higher-income, loan-providing First World citizen. The term *empowerment* operates to create an affective network across citizens from different nations. Consequently, empowerment as a feeling allows the First World lender to ignore the larger social contexts and economic structures that make it necessary to provide that loan.

My examination of these texts demonstrates how, as the rhetoric of women's empowerment moves from one policy to another, it takes on very different meanings, results in differing programmatic initiatives, and therefore has different material consequences depending on the policy's context, history, and geopolitical connections. Through these examples,

I illustrate how a transnational feminist rhetorical analysis that traces a term's interarticulation within policy networks can enable us to better understand the diverse impact of supposedly understood terms and meanings. The diverse texts I examine in this chapter provide examples of the specific sites where we can trace the common, unexpected, and sometimes uneven impact of transnational capitalism on women.

DEFINING EMPOWERMENT: FROM TOP-DOWN TO GRASSROOTS

As I touched upon above, while the concept of women's empowerment has deep roots within late twentieth-century U.S. feminism, it also has a strong foundation within alternative global development models formed by radical feminist critiques of international development policies (Halfon 85). This section lays out a brief history of how the rhetoric of women's empowerment emerged out of the development community's concerns with so-called Third World women's well-being beginning in the 1970s. An understanding of this history is necessary so that readers can see how empowerment rhetorics first materialize and then slowly lose their stability of meaning as varying policy networks employ them.

By situating the Cairo Conference on Population and Development within the Women in Development (WID) and Gender and Development (GAD) movements, I further unpack the feminist empowerment rhetorics within the Cairo Programme of Action so that they may be placed next to subsequent policies that make use of this rhetoric. In doing so, I show how, unlike some policy writers, the Cairo Programme policy writers made recommendations that avoided cultural relativity and colonial power relationships by holistically promoting a pro-woman agenda that addressed a variety of women's circumstances. Additionally, I begin to illustrate how the logic of interarticulation helps us to see how layers of shifting terms support empowerment rhetorics.

The ways in which policy makers initially use the term *empowerment* within the Cairo Programme demonstrates a complex understanding of how a feminist practice of empowerment must embrace grassroots structural, community, political, and personal change while redefining taken-for-granted rhetorics of the family, for example. Ultimately, my goal here is to lay out the initial demand for global women's empowerment rhetorics so that the reader might perceive the necessity of an analysis of interarticulation to observe how empowerment rhetorics circulate successfully within both feminist policy rhetorics and within neoliberal capitalist policy models.

In 1973 the Percy Amendment to the Foreign Assistance Act of 1961 drew Congress's attention to the plight of women from poorer nations. While the notion of women's empowerment was beginning to gain credence within U.S. feminist organizations, as the Percy Amendment demonstrates, a holistic or feminist understanding of the concept itself was still foreign within U.S.-based international policy initiatives; in fact, save for antitrafficking, reproduction, and population policies, the very idea that women had separate needs from men was decidedly absent from international policy until 1973. The amendment's goal, then, is "to give particular attention to those programs, projects, and activities which tend to integrate women into the national economies of foreign countries, thus improving their status and assisting the total development effort" (Integrating Women into National Economies Sec. 203). The amendment also requires "a report from the President concerning the impact of development programs, projects, and activities on the integration of women into the developing economies of countries receiving assistance" (Subsecs. (b) and (c), as added by Public Law 95–88). The Percy Amendment is remarkable for its attempts at integrating women into the mainstream economy and in practice led the way for not only USAID but also supranational organizations to develop programs that would assist women from poorer nations in contributing to their national economies. However, the material practices of the amendment certainly do not embrace or promote a model of empowerment and often the aid intended for women has been confiscated by corrupt governments and used to support crooked political projects. Nevertheless, the Percy Amendment does promote women's needs insofar as it integrates women into the national economy even though it does not promote their personal or communal requirements.

In part due to the Percy Amendment's mandate that U.S. foreign aid take women's particular needs into consideration, a group of university researchers and development specialists from within supranational organizations became increasingly aware of the ways that aid, which was set aside specifically for women, often did not make it directly into the hands of those women (a problem that microloans attempt to address still today). Thus as part of a network of "specialists" from universities throughout the United States and within international aid agencies, WID began to address this crucial disparity. This network noted how traditional development paradigms often overlooked women's place within so-called underdeveloped or developing cultures and tended to ignore how women from these cultures were already contributing to their economies in informal ways.

WID branches within development agencies intended to bring resources directly to women in need and sought to integrate women themselves into development organizations. However, in practice, women from so-called developing nations were not successfully incorporated into agencies such as the World Bank, IMF, or UN; rather, in a large part, U.S. women or women from wealthy European nations tended to take these positions. In addition, WID followed a liberal feminist practice that assumed that as women became formally part of their nation's (and globe's) economy, culturally specific unequal gender relationships would also change. In other words, if women became equal economic partners with men, they would no longer experience gender inequality (see Momsen and Miller; Razavi).[4]

To some extent, because WID focused on women's employment within a traditional linear development model whereby technological advancement, industrial development, and formal labor participation marked a nation's success, WID's methods reflect colonial practices (see Spurr 2–3). Although in the early years WID did not speak directly of women's empowerment, the organization did tend to follow an empowerment model whereby a set of people in power bestowed power onto another group so that they could participate within predetermined "successful" (i.e., Westernized) economic and political structures (see Rowlands 12). Although WID did not intend to promote or support colonial-like practices, because nonlocal women created policies for other women from the top-down, WID advocates were "criticized for a lack of ideological diversity" (especially for not including women of color, poor women, or women from poorer nations on its panels) and for being "too academic, too U.S.

dominated and remote to [represent] . . . gender equality . . . around the world" (Kerr). As Joanna Kerr and Janet Henshall Momsen each further explain, simply integrating women into political structures or within linear development processes did not actually get to the heart of the women's needs from lower-income nations.

As a result, and in part due to the United Nation's Decade for Women, within the 1980s there was a dramatic shift within the scholarly and activist discourses on women and global development toward considering how unequal gender relationships and a lack of local women's voices within development paradigms influence the material consequences of policy. Women from poorer nations began to challenge WID's methods. They saw that WID tended, at once, to focus on individual equity between men and women (a practice that, as I show below, was reified within neoliberal policy models) and homogenize women from different cultures and nations as wanting or needing the same interventions—a practice that, as my earlier chapters show, continued into the twenty-first century.

Critics of WID advocated for a GAD approach to development to confront the ways in which multiple *systems* of social, economic, cultural, and gender norms along with existing development policies and programs disenfranchise women from different nations in differing ways (Halfron 86). This systems approach was key to a GAD philosophy. A GAD approach emphasized that development philosophy needed to incorporate a model of women's empowerment whereby women themselves were equal partners in creating development plans (see Momsen). The GAD movement also noted that empowerment was impossible if women's personal needs were isolated from their community's struggles or the politics that informed those struggles. As a key part to the idea of women's empowerment, GAD recognized that women's well-being was affected by a palimpsest of interlinking circumstances and thus policies that solely promote personal economic development would not alleviate women's disenfranchisement. GAD's empowerment model was also responding to fact that due to the institutionalization of WID within supranational organizations, WID programs had to follow a rational choice model of economic growth. Rational choice philosophy assumes that individuals always act rationally in decision making so that they might achieve the best outcomes for themselves. This economic philosophy promotes policy models that center on individual choices over how choices are constrained by culture, resources, and social and gender norms, to name just a few. As a precursor to neoliberal policies, rational choice economic and development policies for women upheld the thinking that since "discrimination is not economically rational" (Jaquette qtd. in Halfron 86), changing unequal gender relationships will enable women to be fully "rational" economic participants. GAD feminists critiqued WID feminists for focusing mostly on development programs that aimed to bring women into the paid labor market and for homogenizing women's experiences by ignoring the complex social, racial, cultural, and geopolitical aspects of gender inequality and a lack of empowerment (also see Momsen; and Carelton).

For example, Amber Ault and Eve Sandberg's description of the material effects of an IMF development loan to Zambia in the 1980–1990s demonstrates how a GAD systems approach holistically understands women's oppression by highlighting the layered chain of events that affect women in unexpected ways and by drawing attention to how the integration of women into the local and global economies does not always alleviate women's oppression. Their case study also shows how a GAD empowerment model might address Zambian women's circumstances. As part of the parameters of the IMF loan, Zambia was forced to devalue its currency and cut its heavily subsidized health care, food, and education programs.

Although these modifications certainly affected all Zambians because these changes left many citizens with scarce resources and money, they had drastic indirect consequences for women. For example, as a result of these financial constrains, many families chose to send boys to school over girls, and many women also took on triple workdays, often selling goods in the market or working formal jobs to make ends meet while maintaining households and farms. Likewise, women experienced more violence in their homes, as men turned to patriarchal social structures as an outlet for stress, and outside their homes, women became desperate targets of robbery when they went between work, home, and garden (Ault and Sandberg 471). So, while the IMF loan enabled more women to work outside the home, earn an income, and become more integrated into the national economy (a goal of WID), the material results of the loan adversely affected women in unanticipated ways that were remarkably different from men. This example demonstrates the necessity for the GAD empowerment model that moves beyond a focus on bringing women into the mainstream economy; as a result, a GAD approach is interested in promoting an empowerment paradigm that considers the seemingly intangible and unconnected material effects of development policy on women.

Out of the GAD approach's observations and critiques emerged a conceptualization of women's empowerment that seeks to avoid social and economic welfare programs that are top-down oriented or basic needs oriented and instead invites local women to participate actively in grassroots political processes that enable them first to identify their needs and their community needs and then to work toward changing their social, cultural, political, and even personal environment. Ultimately, women use local knowledge, personal experiences, chosen cultural practices, and so forth to define the issues they see as needing to be addressed by policy and then suggest workable solutions that fit with their perceived needs. In returning to the above example of Zambia, GAD feminists might work with women to identify their key concerns, which might be domestic violence or the triple workday over their earning capacity or being integrated into government. In this way, a GAD approach embraces a woman-centered form of empowerment, whereby empowerment is defined by a community, comes from within that community, and is practiced by the women of the community.[5]

EMPOWERMENT AND FEMINISM: A PROGRAM OF ACTION

Although most of the Cairo Programme of Action was drafted in the year prior to the UN Population and Development Conference, the final product is the result of several drafts and complex negotiations between GAD feminists, NGOs, academics, demographers, and economists, to name only a few. Interestingly, the Clinton administration (particularly Timothy Wirth, counselor in charge of population matters in the U.S. State Department) along with several U.S. feminist NGOs were among the principal authors of the Cairo Programme. Their sentiments are reflected both in the focus on (and then redefinition of) cultural institutions like "the family" and in the critiques of neocolonial development policies led by the IMF and World Bank that the Cairo Programme identifies as ignoring women's needs and destroying the local environments that sustain women's work and their families' sustenance. We can further see GAD feminists' influence in their description of empowerment programs that followed the model of Paulo Freire, by including some sort of community-based "conscientization" or "conscious raising" so that individual women would not be mere passive recipients of aid, nor would they be disciplined colonial subjects (Halfron 88). This model of empowerment works against top-down development models and thereby attempts to avoid a (post)colonial power relationship or a dominant development paradigm whereby women are "enlightened" or saved by another entity. By recognizing that women's empowerment is effected by a complex and nuanced relationship between development practices, local culture, gender relationships, and resources (to name only a few factors), the Cairo Programme ultimately promotes women having voice and agency within global policy initiatives that impact their local environment.

While this radical notion of empowerment was explored above in my analysis of the Cairo Programme's introduction, it is also further reflected in chapters two and four of the programme. These chapters additionally interarticulate the kairotic rhetoric of family values into the document's definition of women's empowerment in positive ways. Chapter two of the Cairo Programme, for example, contains the core principles of the document and communicates best practices for supporting a healthy relationship between economic growth, population, and development to nations who have ratified the UN's human rights declarations. Chapter four focuses specifically on women's empowerment (the chapter is titled "Gender Equity, Equality, and the Empowerment of Women") but addresses how, in order for women to be empowered, men also must play a crucial role, policy interventions must be made, the environment must be protected, families must be supported, and women must have agency. Both chapters ultimately demonstrate a GAD influence on the document's conceptualization of women's empowerment.

One of the central focuses of these chapters is on the relationship between women's needs within and outside the home and how those needs relate to family affairs. The way in which the Cairo Programme connects empowerment to women's relationship to their families provides a further example of interarticulation, because within the document the concept of *the family* (which circulated within U.S. policy debates and specifically within the Personal Responsibility and Work Opportunity Act of 1996) shifts as the rhetoric comes to represent a wide range of relationships. For example, Principle 9 states: "The family is a basic unit in society and as such should be strengthened. It is entitled to receive comprehensive protection and support. In different cultural, political and social systems, *various forms of the family exist.* Marriage must be entered into with the free consent of the intending spouses, and husband and wife should be equal partners" (Cairo Programme of Action 13; emphasis added). The way in which the document rhetorically employs the term *the family* is an example of interarticulation because the Cairo Programme reframes the rhetoric so that it encompasses a more holistic view of family structures, and yet due to its timeliness it still resonates with audiences familiar with the term. In addition, the above statement rhetorically links the family to women's empowerment and in doing so, revises the U.S. "family values" rhetoric of the 1990s that I discuss in chapter 2. Despite the fact that the above example makes reference to *husband* and *wife*, it also makes clear that protecting and supporting the family is not limited to heternormative, two-parent structures (as intended in U.S.-based family values rhetoric) but can include extended family, single-parent families, multigenerational families, or even polygamous familial structures if all spouses agree to the relationship. Because the Cairo Programme recognizes that some women come from cultures that rely, for example, on extended family structures to help with care work and farming labor, this redefinition of family becomes part of a rhetoric of women's empowerment that is more inclusive of a variety of women's family structures. By opening up the definition of the family, Principle 9 resists both the colonial practice of promoting particular sorts of heteronormative or nuclear familial arrangements and neoliberalism by noting that the larger community must support families. As I noted in chapter 2, neoliberal policies often use colonial stereotypes and rescue rhetorics as justifications for political interventions. Chapter four of the Cairo Programme also focuses on the relationship between family and work mentioning that the state has a role to play in "making it possible, through laws, regulations, and other appropriate measures, for women to combine the roles of child-bearing, breast-feeding and child-rearing with participation in the work force" (23). Thus, the Cairo Programme recognizes that empowering women entails a symbiotic relationship between individual families, the community, the state, and women themselves.

Chapter four's "Basis for Action" continues to recode family values rhetoric and support women's empowerment by specifically defining the ways in which men and women can sustain each other within heteronormative familial structures—a family structure where unequal power relationships often thrive. It states: "The full participation and partnership of both women and men is required in productive and reproductive life, including shared responsibilities for the care and nurturing of children and the maintenance of the household. In all parts of the world, women are facing threats to their lives, health and well-being as a result of being overburdened with work and their lack of power and influence" (22). Familial relationships are spoken about as a "partnership," and the Cairo Programme further recognizes that women are adversely impacted by the spread of capitalism insofar as despite the fact that more women are working within formal economies, they are still responsible for work within the home. In this example, the rhetoric of women's empowerment is bound to an interarticulated and more pro-woman rhetoric of the family that works to holistically address women's disenfranchisement. Unlike rational choice or neoliberal notions of women's empowerment, within the "Basis for Action" section of the Cairo Programme, women's empowerment extends beyond individual women to include her immediate familial support system alongside her community and nation.

Another central focus is on how women's empowerment is directly connected to broader contexts that stem beyond their personal relationships. Chapter four of the Cairo Programme makes this quite explicit:

> The design of family health and other development interventions should take better account of the demands of women's time from the responsibilities of child-rearing, household work, and income-generating activities. Male responsibilities should be emphasized with respect to child-rearing and housework. Greater investments should be made in appropriate measures

> to lessen the daily burden of domestic responsibilities, the greater share of which falls on women. Greater attention should be paid to the ways in which environmental degradation and changes in land use adversely affect the allocation of women's time. Women's domestic working environments should not adversely affect their health. (24)

The rhetorical connections between women's time, income-generating activities, male responsibility, environmental degradation, and health are remarkable. In this example, the Cairo Programme clearly integrates a GAD analysis of women's oppressions and articulates how her personal, home, and public life coalesce to define empowerment as being able to be free from environmental harm so that women can have control over their time. This nuanced and contextual definition of empowerment is further demonstrated when chapter four connects "women's empowerment" to global policies and the direct and diverse impact such policies have on women's well-being: "Development interventions should take better account of the multiple demands on women's time, with greater investments made in measures to lessen the burden of domestic responsibilities, and with attention to laws, programmes and policies which will enable employees of both sexes to harmonize their family and work responsibilities" (10). In this example, women's empowerment is not provided by mere individual agency, family agency, legal structures, or supranational policies but rather a combination of all these entities. As a result, the Cairo Programme's empowerment model works against rational choice development models that center on the concept of agency through mere personal "choice." While individual agency and the ability to make choices can certainly be a development goal, the Cairo Programme noted that this sort of focus was only warranted when women themselves put forth this goal.

The Cairo Programme is an influential example of women's empowerment; its holistic understanding of women's oppression along with its context specific and diverse pro-woman development model ultimately sets the tone for other policy makers to interarticulate empowerment rhetorics as part of their gender-attendant policy plans. As the term *empowerment* becomes interarticulated into the Beijing Platform for Action, it shifts slightly to expand beyond alleviating culturally derived gender inequalities and toward addressing specific historical and policy practices that exacerbate gender inequities.

EMPOWERMENT: A POST-CAIRO PLATFORM FOR ACTION

Less than a year after the Cairo Population and Development Conference, the UN sponsored the Fourth World Conference on Women in Beijing, China. As discussed in chapter 2, while the conference focused specifically on mainstreaming a gender perspective in national, development, and local policies, this conference also employed the rhetoric of women's empowerment to frame its argument for women's rights as human rights. In fact, the resulting Beijing Platform for Action, another international document that guides nations in best practices for addressing gender inequalities, states in its first line: "The Platform for Action is an agenda for women's empowerment" (*Beijing Declaration* 1). The Beijing conference concentrated on the ways in which women's empowerment related to women's ability to resist impoverishment, participate in public and private decision making, and influence media representations of women and girls. What is particularly significant about the Beijing Platform is how empowerment rhetorics frame gender mainstreaming in ways that are similar to how the Cairo Programme employs the term *empowerment.* While a gender mainstreaming perspective asks policy makers to consider how a policy initiative might affect men and women differently (see chapter 2), empowerment rhetorics in the context of the Fourth World Conference on Women carries a much more nuanced definition thereby offering an example of an interarticulation that is of a similar tone and focus to the Cairo Programme. In the Beijing Platform, empowerment through gender mainstreaming does not simply mean establishing policies that address gender disparities or examining how the policies will impact women and men differently. Rather, the Beijing Platform also employs a holistic definition of empowerment throughout its document that is reminiscent of the Cairo Programme while adding layers to the term's definition.

It notes in its mission statement, for example, how globalization has influenced women's well-being: "Since . . . 1985, . . . the world has experienced profound political, economic, social, and cultural changes, which have had both positive and negative effects on women" (*Beijing Declaration* 3). Among the negative effects that the Beijing Platform mentions are "wars of aggression, armed occupation, civil wars, and terrorism" that often lead to "murder, torture, systematic rape, forced pregnancy and forced abortion" as well as "reduced . . . resources available for social development" (*Beijing Declaration* 3). The Beijing Platform notes that a lack of women's empowerment is not because women and men are different but because gender inequalities (re)produce unjust gendered relationships; these inequalities are often caused by geopolitical and local tensions. In this case, the interarticulated rhetoric of empowerment gently shifts away from a focus on the strains and differences between men and women and on to the external events that produce abject material consequences—war can harm women not only in direct in physical ways but also indirectly through decreased access to resources. Like the Cairo Programme rhetoric of women's empowerment, according to the Beijing Platform, empowerment means developing policies, programs, and practices that do not simply respond to gender inequalities but that actually encourage cultural practices that positively impact women and their diverse needs. Take for example, the third point of the Beijing Platform: "The Platform for Action emphasizes that women share common concerns that can be addressed only by working together and in partnership with men towards the common goal of gender equality around the world. It respects and values the full diversity of women's situations and conditions and recognizes that some women face particular barriers to their empowerment" (*Beijing Declaration* 1). This statement's focus on the "full diversity of women's situations and conditions" demonstrates another layer of interarticulation. While the Cairo Programme clearly understood that in order for development projects or programs to empower women they must consider how broader contextual issues might impact a woman's daily life in unexpected ways, the Beijing Platform adds that although all women are marginalized across cultures, women from different cultures and even women from the same communities might be disenfranchised in very different ways. Likewise, there might be specific cultural practices that may be considered empowering for some women and not for others. The ninth statement in the Cairo Programme demonstrates this very sentiment:

> The full realization of all human rights and fundamental freedoms of all women is essential for the empowerment of women. While significance of national and regional particularities and various historical, cultural, and religious backgrounds must be born in mind, it is the duty of States, regardless of their political, economic, and cultural systems, to promote and protect all human rights and fundamental freedoms. [In addition] each State [must have] full respect for various religious and ethical values, cultural backgrounds and philosophical convictions of individuals and their communities . . . in order to achieve equality, development and peace. (Cairo Programme of Action 3)

The Beijing Platform further demonstrates that women's empowerment is impossible without supporting their culture or religious preferences; likewise, however, it also notes that when women's human rights are violated, it is up to states to intervene. As this example shows, women's empowerment is not simply about shoring up individual women's agency, but rather empowerment is achieved when states, governments, communities, cultures, and women themselves work together to define and then carry out empowerment programs.

Perhaps the most unique part of the Beijing Platform is how the writers demonstrate that development paradigms can in fact be disempowering. The conclusion to the Beijing Platform states: "Accelerated economic growth, although necessary for social development, does not by itself improve the quality of life of the population. In some cases, conditions can arise which can aggravate social inequality and marginalization. Hence, it is indispensible to search for new alternatives that ensure that all members of society benefit from economic growth based on a holistic approach to all aspects of development: growth, equality between women and men, social justice, conservation and protection of the environment, sustainability, solidarity, participation, peace and respect for human life" (*Beijing Declaration* 4). The conclusion's focus on holistic development is key to the Beijing Platform's nuanced definition of empowerment. The Beijing

Platform does not emphasize work and individual choice as subsequent empowerment polices do, but rather it highlights a GAD systems approach to women's oppression and, as such, attempts to articulate how women's empowerment depends upon a matrix of relationships.

EMPOWERMENT IN A NEOLIBERAL CONTEXT

The World Bank had an active and public presence at both the Cairo and Beijing conferences. Yet, soon after the Beijing conference and despite national and international support of women's empowerment initiatives, due to structural adjustment programs and the rise of neoliberal economics, national welfare programs across the globe began to falter, which resulted in uneven national social policies that adversely affected women by widening the economic disparity between men and women. Despite these economic changes, the World Bank openly embraced the concept of women's empowerment and made it one of the organization's core development goals. As I describe in chapter 1, just as low-income and middle-income countries faced significant economic changes, the World Bank named women as the keys to a nation's economic success. However, the empowerment programs and policies that the World Bank conceived looked very much *unlike* the Cairo Programme or the Beijing Platform. In effect, the World Bank stripped away the layered and nuanced definition of empowerment so that the term would reflect the organization's embracement of global neoliberalism, whereby states would have less responsibility for citizen's social welfare and individual citizens would be expected to take responsibility (so to speak) for their economic, social, and physical well-being. Just as the World Bank made a formal commitment to the empowerment of women, many nations with Bank loans and IMF currency devaluation programs had to reduce the very social programs designed to help women navigate an increasingly transnational market system; these programs ranged from basic needs to job training to health care (Rittich 249). Thus, although the World Bank used a rhetoric of women's empowerment, their policies asked many nations to cut maternity, disability, and sickness safety nets and constricted access to family cash allowances, in-kind benefits, and other state-supported social programs.

In the 1990s the World Bank produced several gender attendant policy reports along with quite a few book-length documents in which women's empowerment is interarticulated. It is within these texts that the rhetoric of women's empowerment shifts away from a complex and nuanced understanding of the term *empowerment* as being connected to larger contextual issues to a more superficial definition. These documents demonstrate how rhetorical expectations of language mask political and material realities as women's empowerment comes to mean being a productive and financially independent agent. In other words, the term *empowerment* comes to reflect the neoliberal sentiment that every citizen needs to care for her (and her family's) own welfare. Unlike the Cairo Programme and the Beijing Platform that recognize the cultural specificity of the meaning of family and the diverse and productive ways in which certain communities relied upon and supported families, the World Bank's women's empowerment initiatives follow a neoliberal policy philosophy and focus on making women *less* accountable to their familial and community ties and more responsible for their own personal economic independence. Examining the interarticulations of empowerment rhetorics demonstrates how various institutions effectively employ the term but also how the term's meaning shifts. By investigating the World Bank documents that follow, I show how, as a rhetoric of women's empowerment becomes interarticulated into the Bank's development plans, the phrase moves away from being a productive one to being a potentially destructive one. The World Bank's empowerment rhetorics act as a veil that masks the actual material effects of neoliberal capitalism and policies—such as reduced welfare, health, and job training programs—and in doing so, it elides the political, economic, and personal realities of the women its policies address.

Within the World Bank report *Engendering Development through Rights, Resources, and Voice* the rhetoric of empowerment looks drastically different from the Cairo Programme or the Beijing Platform. *Engendering Development* suggests, for example, that women's subordination is tied to traditional work and lack of contact with modern institutions and markets; these modern institutions and markets will enable women to work outside the home while their families are cared for by other women. The chapter "Gender, Norms, and Customs" describes how some familial structures in South Asia hinder women's ability to achieve personal economic success since "girls leave their natal families when they marry[, and they are] not expected to work for pay in the labor market" (*Engendering Development* 111). The chapter goes on to contrast South Asian families with South American families, arguing that women are more empowered in South American families since their ties to their family are through responsible financial management; the report describes South American women as working outside the home, managing family finances, and providing financial support to elderly parents. The report's practice of holding one region's cultural and material practices as "good" and another's as "irresponsible" reiterates colonial stereotypes of the primitive and unfit against the modern and developed. In this case, the World Bank suggests that women's empowerment is merely attached to a woman's ability to earn and manage money and not to the structural issues that might inform a family's decision to educate a girl or not or to encourage an early marriage or not. Unlike the Cairo Programme or the Beijing Platform, which celebrates several sorts of family structures and notes how women's empowerment is dependent upon support from her nation, state, community, culture, and family, in the above example, empowerment is melded with neoliberal capitalism in ways that elide women's cultural and geopolitical locations. Additionally, the report does not offer a cogent analysis of *why* each region differs. For example, the more recent history of colonialism in Southeast Asia as well as drought or other natural disasters certainly impact a community's overall health. Likewise, the differences might also be read through a gendered labor lens. Do women in South America end up working triple workdays? If so, how has that affected their personal health or their familial relationships? Have Southeast Asian women resisted the move toward marketization and privatization and as such perhaps these women's agricultural labor may not actually be coded as labor despite the fact that it might be what sustains their families? Thus, as the term *empowerment* is interarticulated into this World Bank document, it becomes a mask in which supranational organizations employ neoliberal discourses to further their agendas. By mapping these interarticulations of the term, readers can see how although rhetorics of women's empowerment might appear pro-woman or even feminist, the rhetoric often supports pernicious policies that pit women against each other and ignore the wider contexts in which women survive.

The World Bank's report *Toward Gender Equality*, likewise, explains how social norms (including community ties and traditional familial relationships) are a hindrance to women's empowerment and macrolevel economic development: "Social norms affecting decisions within the family about occupational choices or migration can also lead to differential patterns of male and female earnings in informal markets. Family responsibilities hinder women's geographic mobility, constraining their ability to command high wages" (*Toward Gender Equality* 34). Both reports suggest that if women had access to credit and earned wages, then they could have more bargaining power within the home and the community; this money would create financial and cultural equality between men and women. *Engendering Development* explains, "Women who participate in the credit programs report an increased role in household decision making and greater acceptance by their husbands of their participation in market-based economic activities" (164). In other words, the Bank suggests that gender inequality is not only bad for women but that it also "hinders development" of her nation (*Engendering Development* 73); women, therefore, are key resources for the global economy. As the above examples demonstrate, *Toward Gender Equality* and *Engendering Development* equate women's empowerment with national development (perhaps a nod to the odd adage, "you can judge a nation by how it treats its women") and economic power. This is in direct contrast, for example, to the GAD approach described above where women's empowerment relates to broader contextual issues and not simply to women's ability to have access to money.

The neoliberal logic that credit and markets empower women is enabled by gendered colonial discourses; empowerment circulates as an interarticulated rhetoric that masks women's specific and lived realities. *Engendering Development* defines women's rights as the ability to "own land, manage property, conduct business, or . . . travel without their husband's consent" (4). These basic rights that the report defines are indeed important, but they also resonate strongly with Westernized notions of sovereignty and individualism and stereotypical colonial understandings of Third World women. The terms *own*, *manage*, and *business* collapse the rhetoric of women's empowerment with the rhetoric of neoliberalism; yet the final clause of that list, "travel without their husband's consent," disrupts its entrepreneurial aims. While it is certainly positive for women to travel independently, this short list shows how neoliberal arguments work in tandem with and are furthered by neocolonial ideologies. The Bank reads cultural practices according to the logic of the market; to have to travel with an escort means that a women's market mobility is limited. The cultural context that, in other cases, inform women's choices in examples such as the GAD model of development and within the Cairo Programme and Beijing Platform is discarded in favor of an understanding of empowerment as a kind of personal and (inter)national economic mobility that the market (might) enable.

A section called, "Fostering Economic Development to Strengthen Incentives for More Equal Resources and Participation," in *Engendering Development* further demonstrates how cultural context is disregarded in the World Bank's definition of women's empowerment: "Where active labor markets exist, hired labor provides a substitute for female family labor, whether on farms or in household maintenance or care activities. This allows households to use time more efficiently, perhaps reducing women's workload. Where labor markets are absent or do not function well, such substitution is not possible" (19). This statement exemplifies an important contradiction in the Bank's rhetoric. When markets are present, they provide the opportunity for women, but such opportunities may only benefit some women—to the extent that they can hire other women—and thus they enter into a classed capitalist system. Thus, the capitalist market can only be "empowering" for a certain class of women.

In 2000 (three years after the aforementioned reports were published), the World Bank published another report on the gender attendant programs called *Advancing Gender Equity: World Bank Action since Beijing*; the rhetoric of women's empowerment frames both its foreword and its purpose. The foreword, written by former Bank President James Wolfensohn, claims that since Beijing, the World Bank's "definition of poverty has broadened to address empowerment, security, and opportunity as well as economic growth" (*Advancing Gender Equity* iv). The foreword continues, "In this development environment, the empowerment of women—and of men—has become a central element in the World Bank's strategy for poverty reduction and growth" (*Advancing Gender Equity* iv). Yet, just prior to these claims of understanding how empowering women (and men) can help relieve poverty, the foreword describes a set of issues that impede women's empowerment: "Poor people from across the world suffer from multiple liabilities: lack of food and adequate shelter, victimization by landlords, and a sense of hopelessness in the face of overwhelming odds, to name a few. Gender inequalities add additional costs, not only for women, but children, men, and the society as a whole. We know that domestic violence disables women, leads to a loss of income, increases what a society spends on health care—and unwittingly teaches children to find violent rather than peaceful solutions to problems" (*Advancing Gender Equity* iv). Like the above examples, a lack of women's empowerment is no longer connected to global contextual issues, but rather it is framed as a personal problem—thereby divorcing such problems from the various forms of colonialism that might have engendered the violence. Unlike the case of Zambia (that I describe above) where GAD feminists connect the rise in domestic violence to gross national economic restructuring, here, domestic violence is only seen a hindrance to women's and other citizens' economic well-being and not women's health or to the wider community. This seditious framing thus situates women's empowerment as individual choice and responsibility. As such, the rhetoric of women's empowerment is deployed to eradicate the World Bank and other supranational institutions' culpability. The problem in this case, then, is that a neoliberal logic of hyperindividualism encodes domestic violence as a personal problem, a *woman's* personal problem. Thus, as the rhetoric of women's empowerment becomes interarticulated in these World Bank documents, its meaning shifts to mark women's empowerment as not material and acontextual and merely economic despite the fact that domestic violence, while be tween a group of people living together, is often more likely to happen during times of extreme stress—such as economic instability, during war, and when familial roles shift (as I will make clear below).

The foreword continues to explain that not educating girls leads to fewer opportunities for employment as well as a higher rate of unwanted pregnancies. While all of these observations are indeed true, it is interesting that the World Bank's arguments for empowerment focus specifically on how a lack of empowerment impacts women's ability to be in the paid labor market. As demonstrated above, neoliberal policies often share the colonial logic that changing individual behaviors will reduce poverty and help developing nations enter the global capitalist market. For example, just after the aforementioned statement, the foreword continues, noting that "gender issues . . . also affect men: In many societies with high male unemployment, alcoholism [has] increased rapidly" (*Advancing Gender Equity* iv). In this instance, the foreword depicts men from developing nations as lazy and irresponsible (if not violent). To this extent, men are represented as one of the core impediments to women's empowerment since they commit domestic violence, drink too much, and are unemployed. As I briefly discussed in chapter 2, Kate Bedford observes this very same sentiment in her study of a World Bank gender and development initiative in rural Ecuador. Bedford explores how the policy model sought to "encourage a two-partner model of love and labour wherein women work more and men care better" (295). She describes, for example, how, due to Ecuador's need to expand their export of goods to fulfill the parameters of a World Bank and IMF loan, Ecuador significantly increased its shrimping, palma oil, and wood industries thereby attracting Afro-Ecuadorian men from the midland rural regions to the coasts for work. Yet researchers who have implemented the development policy discovered that the group of men who lived away from their primary families most of the year developed other sorts of familial arrangements and often times had one family on the coast and another within the rural regions of the midland. The Bank found that it was this break in monogamous heteronormative coupling, specifically a lack of familial intimacy—and not the changes to Ecuador's labor market—that led to the Afro-Ecuadorians as a group not succeeding in this new national economy. As Bedford describes, the policy portrays Afro-Ecuadorian men as lazy, drunk, cheating, hypersexual, and irresponsible husbands who do not provide for their families or properly love their wives. In other words, the Bank researchers and subsequently Bank development policy for the region represented Afro-Ecuadorian epistemology as the prime factor in its failure to "develop" a competitive transnational economy and as a hindrance to women's empowerment. Interestingly, Bedford's study crucially reveals that the women she interviewed did not note the nonmonogamous coupling or their male partner's behaviors as their core concerns or needs as the Bank loan documents did. Instead, they noted low-wages and environmental degradation to be their core concerns (Bedford 17).

What is particularly remarkable about the above examples is that colonial stereotypes work in tandem with neoliberalism to advance a definition of empowerment as being tied to productive work and responsible coupling (this representation of women's empowerment is similar to the gendered stereotypes that frame the Personal Responsibility and Work Opportunity Act of 1996 and the PRODEPINE World Bank loan program that I examine in chapter 2). Both *Advancing Gender Equity* and the Bank project Bedford explores demonstrate how the rhetoric of women's empowerment has shifted from a model wherein women (and men) make decisions about their needs to a normalizing model that discounts individual and community desires.

The next section continues to explore the World Bank's promotion of microlending but places this practice within the context of other microfinance industries. While the above examples demonstrates how neoliberalism often works with neocolonialism to justify policy interventions, in the examples that follow, discourses of neoliberalism and neocolonialism join to support an affective rhetoric of empowerment. Yet, because this affective rhetoric appears to support liberal feminist aims, the term masks pernicious power structures that often disenfranchise women.

MICROLENDING: INTERARTICULATING EMPOWERMENT'S NEOLIBERAL AND FEMINIST ROOTS

In 2006 Muhammad Yunus and the organization he founded, the Grameen Bank, won the Nobel Peace Prize for "efforts to create economic and social development from below" through low-interest and non-predatory small loans (or microloans) made directly to individual people (Nobelprize.org). Although Yunus began the Grameen Bank in the 1970s, the idea of microcredit did not gain credence among development experts, NGOs, or supranational organizations until well into the 1990s and 2000s. During the 1980s–1990s, poor nations often faced increased internal governmental corruption and much of the development money loaned for programs to help these nations' poor citizens never made it to those in need. Microcredit loans were, in part, meant to place money directly into the hands of individual citizens in order to bypass corrupt governments. Microlending practices would also allow citizens to articulate their needs by constructing their own business plans that employ their local knowledge.

The most famous Grameen Bank microlending project that has drawn from women's local knowledge is called Village Phones—a program that specifically targeted rural Bangladeshi women. Grameen provided microloans to women in small rural villages in Bangladesh so that they could purchase a mobile phone. Because there were few phones in these villages, the women, who received the loans and then purchased cell phones, would allow other villagers to use their phone for a small fee thereby becoming the "telephone lady" of the village (Grameen Bank). The Village Phones program (as well as many of the Grameen Bank's other microlending programs) follows an empowerment model whereby women, through these very small and low-interest loans, plan, model, execute, and manage their own businesses. Thus, in the discourse and practice of microlending such as the Village Phone program, empowerment rhetorics are interarticulated to link both neoliberal ideologies of personal choice and feminist practices of personal agency within specific cultural milieus.

With the Village Phone project, the goal of women's empowerment has become *the* cornerstone of microlending. Microcredit institutions tend to follow the logic that if women are given the chance to design and then execute their own business plan, women will be empowered not only in the public sphere but also within their own homes where their earning power is thought to neutralize unequal gender power relationships between men and women. In addition, microcredit agencies also argue that when women are able to earn their own money, the health and education prospects of children improve. Thus, the fact that the idea of microcredit and microfinance began to travel among development circles during the same time that the phrase *women's empowerment* circulated and neoliberal policies were legislated is significant.

First, microcredit programs grew alongside neoliberal development policies perhaps because both development paradigms depend upon strong individual agency and choice without the support of government safety nets or in-kind programs. In some ways though, microloans can also be empowering in ways similar to how the Cairo Programme conceptualized empowerment. Individual citizens (or small groups of citizens) employ local knowledge to construct business plans and apply for loans to support those plans. In this way, microloans can also be seen as a grassroots effort.

Yet, in other ways, microloans reflect neoliberal empowerment policy models, because for the loans to work individuals must be self-motivated (and self-reliant). As Robin G. Isserles points out in her exploration of the rhetoric of microlending and her interviews with individuals who work in local microfinance institutions, microlending has become the one size fits all answer to the problems caused by structural adjustment, specifically the unavailability of well-paying jobs, a lack of social services and public-sector employment, and a general growth in poverty (41–42). Moreover, because microlending discourses are steeped with "market populism" (Frank qtd. in Isserles 43), self-reliance, economic independence, and entrepreneurial rhetoric, they hide the larger structural causes of poverty and reify the bootstrap ideology popular in U.S. welfare policies (Isserles 43). Like U.S. welfare policy, microcredit practices make individual behavior central to eradicating poverty (Isserles 45). In addition, because NGOs fund most microloans, governments can rely on microlending agencies to provide some of the services (such as education, job skill development, and health programs) that they had offered prior to imposed neoliberal development policy or structural adjustment programs.

Second, for a variety of reasons, microcredit programs have tended to target women. For example, while Yunus believed that rural women from low-income nations are most adversely affected by poverty and helped the least by larger supranational development industries, other microlending agencies have promoted the idea that women's social capital (or their informal and personal connections to other women) makes them more likely to pay back loans in a timely fashion.[6] Microlending agencies prefer to make loans to groups of women with individual business plans. In many instances, microlending agencies will not provide more loans to individual members of a lending collective until *all* individual loans are paid back. As a result, agencies rely on peer pressure or peer surveillance to make sure each borrower in the community is making the right personal and economic choices to pay the loan back. Jude L. Fernando's interview with a woman who received a microloan in Bangladesh is a good example of how microlending and the rhetoric of empowerment has material consequences; the woman reports that since receiving a microloan, "everybody in the village can tell us what to eat and what not to eat. When we failed to make weekly repayments our group members asked, 'Why did you eat chicken yesterday? Why did you send your son for a movie? Why did you buy new clothes?'" (Fernando 171). This sort of surveillance can be seen as part of a neoliberal policy agenda and neoliberal governmentality since the state becomes less responsible for relations among citizens and citizens must monitor themselves and each other. Unlike the above examples of the neoliberal empowerment programs set forth by the World Bank (and different from the other gender attendant policies I examine in earlier chapters), where women are managed by the state, supranational organizations, or NGOs, microlending agencies tend to promote a model of women's empowerment whereby agencies do not directly manage women's economic behavior but rather employ individual women's personal and local knowledge and connections to conceive of a business plan, execute it, make money, and then pay back the loan.[7]

Yet, at the same time, women may be managed by family, peers, or community members and such supervision can reinforce preexisting gendered, cultural, and sometimes ethnic conflicts. As such, it is important to recognize that microlending practices have mixed material effects for women. As Fernando notes, most studies of the effectiveness of microlending programs focus on repayment of loans. These studies tend to suggest that because women pay back loans and then often apply for new loans, that their material circumstances are improved. Likewise, Isserles recounts that microloans have allowed women a space to network with each other, bettered educational prospects for children, increased the health of communities with microlending agencies, and improved the use of contraception. However, Fernando and Linda Mayoux crucially demonstrate that women who receive microloans often experience increased domestic and community violence, pressure from loan officers and family members to pay back the loan, the burdens of a double or even triple workday, a backlash of gendered traditions, and poverty as they become indebted to the agency. Lastly it is not often clear as to whether women apply for loans at their husbands' demand or not.

Therefore, microlending programs interarticulate empowerment rhetorics in interesting, complicated, and layered ways; and as a result, such rhetorics have varying material outcomes for women: some women may achieve better economic conditions for their families, and others fall into a larger cycle of poverty and violence as Fernando, Mayoux, and Isserles make clear. As Grewal has noted in her employment of a transnational feminist cultural studies perspective (33), within the late twentieth century, liberal feminist discourses draw on a rhetoric of choice to represent (feminist) women's agency (28). She suggests that there are unexamined connections between feminism, consumerism, and notions of (neo)liberal democracy that rhetorically link together within global women's rights campaigns; I suggest that these links can also be found within microlending discourses themselves. Thus, this final section examines how the links between neoliberalism and feminism inform microlending policies and create newly interarticulated empowerment rhetorics that are at once feminist and neoliberal.

The material effects of these newly interarticulated rhetorics illustrate further how the meaning of the term *empowerment* is changeable and not necessarily all positive or all negative. Consequently, when empowerment rhetorics continue to frame microlending policies and programs in the twenty-first century, they become an affective neoliberal practice that attempts to link individuals from low-income nations and high-income nations. The microlending institution Kiva, as will be shown below, interarticulates empowerment rhetorics so that empowerment becomes both a practice and a commonly shared feeling between lenders and borrowers. Like the Grameen Bank, Kiva's empowerment rhetoric supports a neoliberal agenda through its focus on the individual; however, Kiva uses an affective rhetoric of empowerment to enliven individual lenders and situate them as well-intended, activist neoliberal subjects. Within Kiva's lending documents, empowerment operates to create an affective network across citizens from different nations and to some extent allows the First World lender to survey and exoticize the people to whom they loan, but these documents also give the lower-income citizen the agency to speak back to their lender.

"WE LET YOU LOAN TO THE WORKING POOR": MICROLENDING'S VIRTUOUS SPIRAL OF EMPOWERMENT

Five years post Beijing, in *Advancing Gender Equality*, the World Bank notes that both credit and savings programs are part of the overall movement to empower women and to combat poverty. In *Advancing Gender Equality*, the Bank cites examples of how their microlending programs have employed the Beijing Platform's philosophy by connecting the results of microfinance with key goals such as "increased schooling for both girls and boys, greater participation by men and women in the labor market, and more assets (other than land) held by women" (7). One of the most notable examples of World Bank–supported microlending is the Velugu project in Andhra Pradesh, Pakistan. Velugu (which means "light" in Telugu) is a unique program that, according to its World Bank planning document, seeks to fight poverty through the formation of grassroots "self-help" groups.[8] The planning document describes how "organizing the poor into self-managed[, s]elf-help Groups … and developing the social capital in the form of activists, paraprofessionals etc., from within the community, [will help the poor in their] collective efforts to overcome their social, economic, cultural and psychological barriers from the basic elements of social mobilization" (World Bank, "Andhra Pradesh District Poverty Initiatives Project [Velugu]" 5).

The planning document is significant due to the conflation of empowerment as self-help and self-management alongside a focus on community. This example demonstrates what Grewal has noted as an interarticulation of empowerment rhetorics as including neoliberal and feminist ideologies. As a World Bank newsletter that reported on the Velugu project further explains, "self help groups (SHGs) of very poor women . . . create collective economic enterprises and social action committees that empower the group members. A key principle of the program is that sustainable poverty eradication requires the poor to be equal partners in social change. For this reason, all Velugu's interventions are demand based and respond to proposals conceived and planned by the poor ("Collective Enterprise and Action"). In both these examples, the words *collective*, *social action*, and *equal partners* suggests a grassroots and feminist approach to microlending. These terms support microlending's rhetoric of empowerment by making it seem as what Mayoux describes as a "virtuous spiral" of empowerment: "increased economic empowerment, improved well-being and social/political/legal empowerment for women" (959). In other words, women who have received microloans are in total awareness and control of the lending process— they work *with* microlending agencies; they are activists in the movement for poverty eradication; they are in charge of their destinies.

Yet, within both these reports, the term *self* also links to the term *empowerment* and as such shifts attention away from larger contextual issues such as local, gender, political, and cultural structures. The notion of self-help empowerment borrows from the language of popular psychology and thus suggests that the poor are not poor due to extenuating circumstances beyond their control, but rather they are poor because they need to work on themselves, implying that they do not have the correct mind-set to pull themselves out of impoverishment. In addition, as the rhetoric also advocates, women are empowered merely by their own tenacity and cleverness to identify community needs and then articulate a workable plan to profit from these needs. In the above examples, changing behavior (both individual and group) becomes the central way that women from a low-income nation will come out of poverty and be empowered.

The idea that individual impoverishment is due to behavior is further supported in the conclusion to the "Promising Approaches to Gender and Development" report on the Velugu project when the article states: "[Self-help] Group members express greatly increased self-confidence and a sense of empowerment through their collective actions. Evaluations show that project activities have led to increases in poor people's capital and freedom of choice; better access to markets and business services; and easier access to the justice system." In this example, the rhetoric of empowerment has a distinctly condescending tone as the report suggests that before the presence of the microloan and its accompanying self-help format, women were meek, did not trust themselves, and were unable to be creative agents. In this case, neoliberalism works with colonial stereotypes that assume that women from poor nations are not self-confident, nor are they able to exercise choices. Interestingly, in Isserles's research on how women fare after receiving microloans, she found that women often report that microenterprise organizations tend to assume that poor women need to be taught how to be active agents when, in fact, due to their impoverished situation, poor women are often both strong advocates for themselves and their families and are more responsible due to the precarious position of being poor (44).[9]

The report's focus on the fact that "group members express greatly increased *self-confidence* and a *sense* of empowerment" (emphasis mine) adds an affective layer to the rhetoric of women's empowerment. This notion of self-consciousness is also reminiscent of images within older *National Geographic* magazines where a journalist holds up a mirror in front of the represented "exotic native" so that he or she can see himself or herself seemingly for the first time. Catherine Lutz and Jane Collins in their analysis of such images suggest that the practice of showing the "native" to himself or herself reflects older colonial practices whereby Christian missionaries attempted to show colonial subjects that they have a soul. While the above example is not showing women their souls per se, the rhetoric suggests that if women were more self-aware, if they could *feel* how they were being empowered, then they are more likely to have the confidence to be out of poverty. Moreover, coupled with the rest of the report, in this example, women must not only be self-aware, active, and self-reliant economic agents, but they must also be empowered women who are in touch with their feelings. Such a focus on the self and a felt sense of empowerment further interarticulates neocolonial, neoliberal, and feminist ideology into women's empowerment rhetorics. Empowerment is no longer a tangible practice but a personal *feeling*, a *sense*. While having a sense of personal empowerment is part of Hill Collins's conceptualization of feminism, this interarticulation of empowerment reflects a Western notion of the self by connecting self-awareness to rational self-management and uncoupling feelings and the self from broader political and cultural constructs (Rose and Miller 143).

Empowerment as a feeling along with the self-help rhetoric of the Velugu project further supports a neocolonial and neoliberal idea of hyper–self-management taught by expert lenders who relate to their client or borrowers in a "pedagogic and responsibilizing form" (Rose and Miller 106). So-called unempowered women are seen as individuals who are not fully formed agents because they do not have a sense of self-awareness necessary to become rational self-reliant actors in transglocal capitalism. Thus, the Velugu project focuses on "the cognitive, emotional, practical and ethical skills [necessary] to take personal responsibility for rational self-management" (Rose and Miller 106). Accordingly, as Michael Rose and Peter Miller describe, "empowerment, then, is a matter of experts teaching, coaxing, requiring their clients to conduct themselves within particular cultural communities of ethics and lifestyle, according to certain specified arts of active personal responsibility" (106). The very notion of selfhood and empowerment as sensed becomes a necessary part of capitalism.

A rhetoric of empowerment as a sensed feeling also frames the innovative microlending organization Kiva. But Kiva has interarticulated the rhetoric of women's empowerment to also mean empowerment as a practice. Kiva's lending procedures are different from other microlending agencies because they invite everyday citizens from higher-income nations to invest their own personal funds directly to individual women from lower-income nations. Their website's motto is "We let you loan to the working poor," and their mission is "to connect people through lending for the sake of alleviating poverty" ("What is Kiva?").[10] Kiva uses the term *empower* not only to describe what the loans will do for those who receive them but also for those individual people who loan money. They state, "Kiva is the world's first person-to-person micro-lending website, empowering individuals to lend directly to unique entrepreneurs around the globe" ("What is Kiva?"). On their website, empowerment as a practice and feeling is made possible through money transferred from lender to borrower, creating a seemingly affective connection between the two.

In a model that is similar to Save the Children, where people can give money and sponsor a child (although the money does not necessarily go directly to that child), Kiva works by allowing individuals to select an entrepreneur from poor parts of the world to give a loan to for as little as twenty-five dollars, creating "a similar interpersonal connection" ("What is Kiva?"). In exchange, lenders receive online updates about the people they loan to. Kiva promotes this back-and-forth relationship and claims that "through Kiva, our partners upload their entrepreneur profiles directly to the site so you can lend to them. When you do . . . you get a unique experience [of] connecting to a specific entrepreneur on the other side of the planet" ("What is Kiva?"). The communication between lenders and borrowers enables an affective connection for the lenders, allowing them to feel empowered by providing a loan.

Kiva's empowerment rhetoric can be read in several ways; to some extent, Kiva appears to reify empowerment rhetorics in ways similar to the World Bank. Certainly, we can read the neocolonial, neoliberal, and feminist undertones of the term: lenders become empowered by seeing (or surveying) how borrowers use their loans; Kiva, as a microlending institution, centers on individually designed and executed business plans, calls borrowers "entrepreneurs," focuses on economic independence, and lenders become business partners with borrowers; and, Kiva enables borrowers to articulate their own (and their community's) needs through their website. Yet, unlike the examples from the Velugu project, whereby empowerment is a learned and decontextualized feeling, Kiva's employment of empowerment as a feeling and practice begins to shift away from neoliberal and neocolonial connotations of the term in important ways.

While the Velugu project focuses on a sense of empowerment as being a teleological effect of transnational capitalism, Kiva's lenders feel empowered not only by making a loan but also through their correspondence with borrowers. Empowerment in this context shifts the power relationship between higher- and lower-income nations. While empowerment, to this extent, is bequeathed from one to another, it is the lower-income borrower who empowers the higher-income lender. Moreover, the fact that the borrowers design and execute their own entrepreneurial projects means that the high-income lender has no control over the project; the lender merely supplies the capital. Although Mayoux questions microlending's "virtuous spiral of empowerment," I suggest that Kiva does provide a spiral of empowerment from the bottom up and thereby draws attention to how so-called First World lenders have a mutually beneficial relationship with so-called Third World borrowers. Kiva's program delinks lending from neocolonialism and enables this spiral of empowerment by facilitating cross-cultural communication through their website. This interaction gives borrowers a chance to speak back to lenders and tell them about their project, ask for more loans, and explain how their project relates to the local circumstances of their community. This sort of cross-cultural, back-and-forth conversation shows potential of new understandings of empowerment and makes possible a new sort of economic development whereby borrowers are not managed by their lenders; rather, lender and borrower can participate in development as partners—one who benefits materially (i.e., they have access to more financial resources) and another who benefits emotionally.

As Kiva's practices and promotional materials show (and indeed, as all the above examples demonstrate), even within a single context, the term *empowerment* is not static but always changing. In one instance empowerment can be read as a neocolonial and neoliberal practice, in another empowerment is a shared feeling, and in still another, empowerment is enabled by learning from those without much power, the low-income borrower. This constant shifting and interarticulation demonstrates the potential of empowerment rhetorics to not only work on a grassroots level (as a GAD approach promotes) but also on affective level that links the citizens from low-income nations to high-income nations. Ultimately, this rhetoric of empowerment shifts power by opening up the possibility that the person providing the loan may actually have something to learn from the person taking a loan. This rhetoric of empowerment then might also provide the opportunity for the wealthy lender to look critically at her or his place in the global economy.

So, while Saul Halfon is correct in his description of empowerment as being a "free floating signifier," and the *Wall Street Journal* reporter is apt in his recognition of the difficulty of translating the concept of women's empowerment, by reading for rhetorical interarticulations, feminists can begin to see and lay bare the diverse and intricate ways that rhetorics collect contextual palimpsests of history, culture, and politics that influence meaning. By unpacking such intricacies and accounting for rhetoric's multidimensionality, we can account not only for what the term masks but also for its possibilities for a better understanding of global inequalities.

Due to the currently unfolding economic crisis and due to the limited sorts of information we receive about poor women across the globe, networking microtexts (such as the rhetoric of empowerment) to macrocontexts is necessary for developing transnational feminist reading and writing practices. These practices help move us toward critically examining our own literacies about poor women who reside in impoverished nations and, crucially, to identify all of the networks that create local instances of poverty and exploitation. Without a transnational feminist literacy, we will continue to make policies that do not address the multiple and networked reasons that women and other minorities continue to be among the poorest of the poor.

AFTERWORD

Networking Arguments as a Writing Process for the New Millennium

THROUGHOUT this book I have demonstrated how feminist rhetoricians might track networked arguments to account for the impact of globalization and global neoliberalism on women. I have offered a transnational feminist rhetorical methodology that shifts current studies in feminist rhetorics from analyzing not only specific women's (or groups of women's) rhetorical acts to how networks of global institutions, supranational organizations, and nation-states shape women's lives through policy arguments; these arguments often simultaneously draw upon historical pretexts and emerging ideologies about productivity in a global economy. *Networking Arguments* also shows how the dissemination of these arguments can constrain and enable women to speak, be heard, and have agency.

My transnational feminist network model emphasizes that the identity category of "woman" is entangled within a variety of powerful linkages. Thus, in order to understand women's oppression, feminist rhetoricians must consider not only a woman's local circumstances but also how vectors of power—supranational policies, colonial history, global economic structures, and even our practices here in the West—shape women's lives in disparate places. In other words feminist rhetoricians must place microexamples within macrocontexts. This new method of feminist rhetorical analysis pays attention to how arguments about women travel, shift, and change and also illustrates that we must pay attention to these shifts in arguments, not just the arguments themselves. In doing so, my analysis moves us toward a better understanding of the uneven impact of globalization on women as I demonstrate how arguments about women in our contemporary global economy often say more about the contexts in which policy makers, supraorganizations, and NGOs structure development programs and policies than about specific women.

I enact this methodology by tracing three central recurring terms that emerged and circulated within late twentieth-century global gender policies and development initiatives—mainstreaming, fitness, and empowerment—in order to show how, as these rhetorics travel, their meanings shift and change depending upon the contexts in which they are used and upon who is using them. Drawing from transnational feminist theory, I redefine three terms (transcoding, ideological traffic, and interarticulation) as rhetorical concepts that illustrate how rhetorics are not static but affected by relationships of power. I suggest that by tracing the process of transcoding, feminist rhetoricians can note how rhetorical meaning is not stable and how wider global processes and contexts can affect rhetorical meaning. In doing so, I make clear how the rise of neoliberalism, specifically, impacts how policy makers transcode their arguments about women's place in the global economy. Likewise, I demonstrate the importance of networking arguments to the past. I look at documents across a single occasion by examining the ideologies that traffic in arguments, noting how these arguments can evoke dangerous historical discourses within progressive-looking policies. At the same time, by tracing ideological traffic, we can note when arguments fall apart and offer conjunctural moments of possibility—helping us reimagine political, economic, and global arrangements. Finally, I ask rhetoricians to consider how arguments become interarticulated with a network of relationships that impact a rhetoric's transnational circulation by tracing how rhetorics and power move. Interarticulation as a rhetorical concept can help us account for the shifting meanings and unevenness of rhetorics as they travel in international development programs. Interarticulation also addresses the wide-range effects of globalization and highlights the complexities of global realities as well as the *diverse* material effects of globalization on women—including positive effects. By noting interarticulations, we can detect the emancipating possibilities of rhetoric.

This work, then, extends current feminist rhetorical studies by looking not at women's individual rhetorical acts but rather arguments about women *and* how arguments about women travel. Most work in feminist rhetorical studies focuses on a woman's rhetorical acts within a particular time period, within a single occasion. I extend a transnational feminist lens to the study of rhetoric by demonstrating the need to trace the circulation of arguments about women and to look not only at these arguments themselves but how those arguments network to wider contexts such as historical discourses, geopolitics, global economics, and cultural expectations. While historical recovery is an important part of feminist rhetorical study, these studies often do not consider how vectors of power affect the arguments that are written about women; they do not consider how past and present geopolitical and economic arrangements can be exigencies for particular arguments about women.

As a result, *Networking Arguments* offers a specifically feminist rhetorical method, which is different from traditional rhetorical methods that examine the relationship between speaker, text, and audience in specific historical moments. I look not just at static rhetorical occasions but how rhetorics move across occasion, time, space, and geopolitical location. To perform a transnational feminist rhetorical methodology we must not look only at women's rhetorical acts but also how power and the circulation of rhetorics affect how women are represented and then consider how women are both constrained and enabled by these representations. In other words, feminist rhetorical analysis must account for how power operates through, and then is sometimes masked by, arguments, persuasion, and circulation. My transnational feminist rhetorical analysis shows how contemporary globalization affects enactments and scales of power and the circumstances of persuasion generally and policy arguments about poor and Third World women specifically.

The rhetorics I trace in this book (mainstreaming, fitness, and empowerment) have been celebrated by the global development community as being part of a pro-woman and, even at times, feminist discourse. However, using a transnational feminist rhetorical method, I show, by looking at the broader transmission and employment of these rhetorics, that we can see how such rhetorics are often used to support development initiatives that reinforce, retrench, augment, and even extend the very power structures that adversely impact poor women in the first place. Thus, *Networking Arguments* suggests that feminist rhetoricians must consider power through an exploration of how policy rhetorics are linked—how they are disseminated, received, rewritten, and put in action—in unexpected ways. At the same time, I also show that because rhetorics are malleable, we can work to redefine them to expose the connections between rhetoric and the material. Drawing from transnational feminist theory and practice, I analyzed these often hidden linkages to show readers both the oppressive *and* promising rhetorics that frame international discourses on women and other minorities.

Crucially, however I want to make clear that networking arguments is not just an analytic process that demonstrates the relationship between power and persuasion. Rather, networking arguments is also a writing process that compositionally exposes the linkages among power, wider contexts, and rhetorical meaning. I suggest that it is through networking arguments in our writing and reading practices that our scholarship and teaching can, in due course, lead to more thoughtful public policies and development programs that critically engage and link together geopolitics, history, and local circumstances so that women and other minorities are not managed. Policy and development must address multiple scales of disenfranchisement.

So, while throughout this book I have demonstrated networking arguments in several ways, I wish to end by briefly showing how networking arguments can be a method of reading and writing—a method, that is necessary for the global milieu of the new millennium, where at once we face a global economic crisis that has disproportionately affected women and children from the poorest nations in the world. In many ways, this crisis has opened an opportunity for us to hear from and learn about people affected by this crisis; this is both promising and concerning because of the sorts of stories we hear and how they might trigger our preconceived notions about poor women, their agency, and our roles as wealthy people in a globalized economy.

Thus we need networking arguments to be a reading and composing practice that makes connections between entities, places, practices, and histories that might at first appear to not relate to each other. When writing networked arguments then, feminist rhetoricians might draw connections between, for example as I do in this book, economic philosophies, geopolitical and local histories, as well as cultural expectations. They might also note how these vectors affect their own study of rhetoric and what they choose to analyze or not.

Looking across my chapters, for example, the Beijing Platform and the Cairo Programme offered written networked arguments when the guiding documents define mainstreaming and empowerment not as undefined and empty terms but rather as discursive practices that make connections between women, their local material environments and cultures, their nation's history, their personal needs, the global economy, and the practices of supranational institutions. In other words, both the Cairo Programme and the Beijing Platform network their arguments by drawing attention to these various vectors of power and how those vectors impact women's lived experiences. These documents make clear that each woman's circumstance is transnationally networked to the economic, social, and political conditions of contemporary neoliberalism, neocolonialism, and neoimperialism and that women, as a category, do not have monolithic identities. When writing, feminist rhetorical scholars might similarly network their arguments by considering how local culture, history, personal desire, the economy, and geopolitics impact women's rhetorical acts across time and place.

To write networked arguments ultimately means connecting the micro and the macro by situating writing practices within far-reaching economic and political systems and by drawing connections between vectors of power: state and supranational power, rhetorical representations, history, class relations, and sexual, gendered, raced, and ethnic identity. Networking arguments is thus not just an analytic but also a material practice. Networking arguments can result in writing projects that influence how, for example, policy makers understand that what appears to be the local situations of particular women are actually due to global economic changes.

I am ultimately urging rhetoricians to pay close attention to the micro within the macro—looking at how small instances of texts relate to larger global economic, political, and cultural movements—when they write (networked) arguments. Networking micro arguments to the macro contexts has become increasingly more important for our present cultural milieu of neoliberalism (economic, political, and cultural) where choice and investment are conflated with agency and where an exorbitant amount of information is at once readily available via the far reaches of the internet but also constrained by our own personal choices in that access (see Richard Miller and Lisa Duggan).

CONNECTING THE MICRO AND MACRO: A CALL TO WRITE NETWORKED ARGUMENTS

This book was completed in the middle of a global financial crisis—a crisis that makes clear how intertwined our material well-being is with other countries and vice versa. As such, this crisis has made the general public more aware of how the local microstories of job loss relate to macro global economic systems; they see how the local and global exists in a complex network. At the very least, people are experiencing firsthand that job loss in one country impacts production and then jobs in another and that moving manufacturing jobs overseas has lowered prices of products for many high-income nations but the citizens of these nations are left with unstable job prospects that do not offer living wages or benefits. In fact, this crisis to an extent demonstrates the need for networking arguments to trace *how* our practices here impact others in faraway places.

This crisis, coupled with war in the Middle East and the more recent natural disasters such as the tsunami in Southeast Asia and Japan and economically, socially, and culturally debilitating earthquakes in India and Haiti, has significantly shifted how development experts have thought about the best practices for economic development. Just after the earthquake in Haiti and in response to the global economic crisis, for example, National Public Radio aired a special report on how the IMF has changed its development strategies in light of this global crisis. According to the report, the IMF openly recognizes that the free market and neoliberal ideology that it has promoted for decades is failing to address the vast needs of low-income countries and their citizens. Due to the current economic crisis and in light of the financial challenges lower-income nations such as Haiti face, the IMF now notes "developing countries might benefit from controlling how much foreign capital enters their economies —and how it's used" (Gjelten). Likewise, in a recent *Reuters* report, the World Bank chief Robert Zoellik stated that "the old concept of 'Third World' no longer applies and rich countries cannot impose their will on developing nations that are now major sources of global growth" (Wroughton). As these two most influential development organizations note, such disasters have posed new challenges for the development community, especially since both have affected nations' economies and abilities to pay back development loans or put into practice development initiatives. While I am unsure about how the IMF and World Bank (and other supranational organizations, for that matter) will change their development and lending practices, not to mention their political commitments, perhaps this financial crisis will make it clear to such organizations that it is imperative to see impoverishment and development through a networked lens, that is, to realize that development needs to look at each nation (and even each community) from a variety of perspectives so that they realize that neoliberal, one size fits all, poverty to work programs do not bring a nation and its citizens out of poverty. Perhaps they will use the technique of networking arguments in their development plans and policies, thereby creating more holistic programs that respond to the particular needs of citizens and nations and that are wary of powerful local and global interests. Regardless, this crisis and these natural disasters demonstrate further the necessity for feminist rhetoricians to examine how women and their needs are represented and to examine what happens to the rhetorics that circulate as the global community rethinks development initiatives.

Optimistically, due to these occurrences more people have become interested in what is happening outside the borders of the United States and Europe. We see this through the publishing of fiction and nonfiction books, films, and television shows that address issues like war and ethnic cleansing in Sierra Leone and Sudan, immigration, rape, female genital surgeries, dowry murder, and veiling to name only a few. As an example, recently, Knopf Press published the book *Half the Sky: Turning Women's Oppression into Opportunity* written by the Pulitzer Prize–winning and humanitarian journalists Nicholas Kristof and Sheryl WuDunn. *Half the Sky* tells stories about individual women from across the developing world. Perhaps due to this global economic crisis and these recent environmental catastrophes that have brought the so-called Third World into the living rooms via television, computer screens, and radios of the so-called First World, the book has had a strong and uncritical reception in the United States. A special issue of the *New York Times Magazine* accompanied the book's release and the editor of this special issue, ignoring the history of feminist organizing for women's rights globally as well as the rise of the Women in Development (WID) and Gender and Development (GAD) paradigms I discuss earlier in the book, suggests that Kristof and WuDunn have begun a new crusade for women's rights in the developing world. Likewise, popular media outlets ranging from the *New York Times* to *Reuters* and then even feminist media organizations such as the blog *Feministing* and the magazine and website *Bitch* have praised the book for exposing the gendered violence—or "gendercide" as Kristof and Wudunn call it in their book—that women continue to face in Third World countries in the twenty-first century.

Each of these reviews thoughtfully drew attention to the fact that the *Half the Sky*, through microstories of individual women, exposes heinous problems of violence against women and girls throughout many parts of the world, including sexual slavery, trafficking for prostitution, dowry murders, rape, and acid attacks, to name only a few. These stories, as the *New York Times* points out, do put a human face on the struggles that women from lower-income nations face through close-up and intimate details of individual women's lives. And, through these microstories, Kristof and WuDunn certainly offer a sort of pro-information literacy campaign about how, in some lower-income countries, women face gendered oppressions and gendered violence both in the private and public sphere. In all cases, each story ends on a hopeful note and each of the women the book portrays are helped by either a microloan (where they start a business), education, or by Kristof himself (literally saving "brown women from brown men"). Kristof and WuDunn do show, how across lower-income countries, women face gendered oppressions. In doing so, the book makes a valuable case for the fact that much of the violence that women cope with goes unreported, especially in mainstream media outlets, or if reported, such events do not register as *gendered* violence. Thus, to this extent, the book should be commended for offering information about women's struggles in places that are often discounted in common, everyday reporting.

Yet, I find this book's popularity and the way in which this book is written troubling precisely because it does not network arguments and especially because in an era of financial crisis we need to recognize how the local and global are completely intertwined and have distinct material effects on women. While *Half the Sky* and its authors have made the public more aware of how violence is gendered, they do not offer any real solutions to the problems nor do they offer a cogent analysis of how audiences might holistically understand problems that women face—they do not network each women's story to wider contexts. In fact, like many of the documents I analyze in earlier chapters, they often resort to old colonialist stereotypes of Third World women as passive and meek to justify neoliberal practices that promote personal responsibility, tenacity, and will.

As a result, in *Half the Sky* each story of an individual woman (coming from a low-income nation) becomes a metonymic representation of all women who reside in the Third World; each woman becomes an argument for neoliberal gender mainstreaming, economic fitness, and personal empowerment. Take for example the story of Srey Neth, a teenager that Kristof and WuDunn purchase and then set free from a Cambodian brothel. At Neth's request, Kristof and WuDunn return her to her family and provide her money to open a small village grocery story. Once Neth is back with her family, she opens her store, which ultimately fails when her relatives raided it for a family feast and refused to pay for the items they took. According to the book, Neth decides then to become a beautician and does so with the support of the American Association for Cambodia. Neth's story ends happily and normatively heterosexual, as she is married, HIV-negative, and has a son. While Neth's story appears as one of freedom and empowerment, it is also a story that obfuscates other unhappy stories because it does not address a more complex view of sex work as a result of several factors. Neth's story is just one of many that *Half the Sky* tells and reflects the dominant narrative of progress present in all the stories. Neth, through a personal loan, seemingly becomes empowered, fits into a global economy, and is a coherent and productive citizen who through her own personal tenacity (indeed Kristof and WuDunn recount how Neth's winning personality and outgoingness help her thrive) appears a part of a successful economic mainstreaming initiative. I do not doubt that Neth's life was saved by Kristof and WuDunn's efforts; but Neth is just *one* of many young women who are trafficked each year.

Kristof and WuDunn's efforts will not stop the *systemic* trafficking of women and girls because they do not address the networks of sex work; they are not addressing the network of macro conditions that make human trafficking possible, and they are not unpacking or connecting these macroconditions to the microconditions (such as the ideologies of race and gender) that work on a local level. Like all the examples in the *Half the Sky*, Neth's story begins sadly and ends happily and thus allows readers to forget the macro in this microstory. Kristof and WuDunn's efforts do not draw attention to *why* Neth was trafficked in the first place.

Yes, the authors explain that Neth was kidnapped and sold by her cousin, but what we do not know is *why* she was kidnapped. Surely it is not just because this cousin (or all Cambodians, for that matter) do not respect women or family. What if we looked closer at the history of the region? There is plenty of literature about how political and military instability and violence have contributed to the economic conditions that created large markets for sex work in Cambodia, Vietnam, and Thailand (see for example, Enloe). Sex work tends to proliferate around military bases. How did the Khmer Rouge (along with the United States', Thailand's, and Great Britain's support of it) impact the nation's economy? The nation's view of gender roles? Its policies? Its local ethnic struggles? What is Cambodia's education system like? Has Cambodia taken loans from the IMF? If so, what sort unintended ramifications have those loans caused? What if we think about how Cambodian women tend to be represented? How are women in Cambodia marketed as exotic, erotic, and supplicant (i.e., broader ideologies of Asian womanhood)? Thailand and Cambodia have become tourist destinations; how do these sorts of images of women attract tourists to visit and take part in illicit sexual activities? How are tourists complicit with human trafficking?

These are the sorts of questions one might ask in order to *network* Neth's story to wider cultural, political, historical, and economic issues. Although *Half the Sky* offers awareness, an audience's response to it is limited because the book does not network arguments; because it does not look at specific histories of specific countries; because it does not consider geopolitics; because it does not consider how lending practices have decimated national economies; and, because it does not ask us to place a critical lens on our own practices. What *Half the Sky* does ask from wealthy high-income women and men is for a limited response and band-aid response: to donate money. But why as feminist rhetoricians should we care? I believe we have the tools to offer new ways of reading, understanding, and responding to popular texts like these.

Through a transnational feminist rhetorical approach we can identify how *Half the Sky* as a rhetorical narrative as well as its composition relies on microstories that often mask macrolevel power relationships. These stories, while compelling, ultimately hide the material and structural causes that allow or constrain women's rhetorical engagement and, ultimately, their autonomy. Despite these critiques and my troubles with the book, I do not want to throw the baby out with the bathwater. Rather, I suggest we might look productively and critically at *Half the Sky* to find its fissures so that we can formulate new responses and actions. Books such as this that offer microinstances give us an opportunity to fill in the blanks of each story. In other words, *Half the Sky* offers us a pedagogical moment to analyze what sorts of arguments the text makes and what sorts of arguments move us toward (limited) action. It, in the end, provides an example of why feminist rhetoricians need to embrace transnational feminism and the practice of networking arguments.

Books like *Half the Sky* let wealthy audiences from wealthy nations in particular avoid thinking through power relationships, but as feminist rhetoricians we can lay bare these power relationships by writing alternative stories. A transnational feminist rhetorical practice that analyzes networked arguments helps us imagine new possibilities for addressing wider contexts.

Ultimately, we stand at a kairotic moment that is an exigency for networking arguments: an opportunity for rhetoricians to think about their own writing practices, to consider how their arguments may be complicit with broader social, historical, and economic practices. To return to the epigraph I began this book with, "Global connections are everywhere. So how does one study the global?" We might answer it by saying, let's network arguments—let's pay attention to the inconsistencies and incoherence; let's see how and why rhetorics move and change; and finally, let's connect the relationships among persuasion, language, power, circulation, and contexts.

NOTES

CHAPTER ONE. NETWORKING ARGUMENTS

1. The term *supranational* refers to policies or organizations that transcend or extend beyond national borders, interests, or spheres of influence. The European Union and the World Trade Organization are two examples of supranational organizations.

2. In John Trimbur's essay "Composition and the Circulation of Writing" he notes (following Stuart Hall) the importance of exploring "passages of form" as writing circulates. Trimbur uses the example of breast cancer information and asks students to trace how scientific findings circulate in a variety of documents. He claims that writing teachers ought to attend to circulation "and, in effect, how [information or rhetoric] is exchanged and capitalized" (203), noting that these "rhetorical transformations . . . occur as a 'passage of forms,'" "transformations that take place between the various specimens of writing make up a total system of production" (213). As I will further explicate in this chapter, my theory of networking arguments builds upon Trimbur (among others, including transnational feminists) thinking about the circulation of rhetorics as it relates to the *conditions* of circulation.

3. Neoliberal ideologies, economic plans, and policies generally share the logic that the privatization of social services, the workings of the market, and changing individual behaviors will reduce poverty and help developing nations enter the global capitalist market. I discuss neoliberalism as a rhetorical occasion and as a global governmentality further in this chapter and throughout the book.

4. Scholars of globalization have tended to examine how economic, cultural, and discursive practices reify hierarchal structures such as the dominance of the First World over the Third World; yet, such analytic assumptions can be totalizing and they work against transnational feminist thinking. Michael Hardt and Antonio Negri's book *Empire* is one of the first to claim that global dominance is not tied to one or a set of nation states; they state "in this smooth place of Empire, there is no *place* of power—it is both everywhere and nowhere. Empire is an *ou*-topia, or really a *non-place*" (190). Although Hardt and Negri have been criticized by postcolonial scholars for throwing the nation out with the bathwater (see Cooppan, for example), their argument does demonstrate an alternative understanding of how global power dynamically circulates across and within nation-states, through supranational organizations so that the First and the Third Worlds (so to speak) may not in fact be territorialized but enmeshed. Hardt and Negri's argument, however, appears ungrounded because it does not provide detailed evidence of how Empire works on a material level nor does it demonstrate the specific examples of how the workings of Empire work translocally. Hardt and Negri's concept of Empire ignores the very unique and subtle spaces where empire is challenged: through feminist NGOs, grassroots movements, the microlending institutions, and labor protests, to name just a few.

5. Sanjeev Khagram and Peggy Levitt suggest that transnational studies scholarship differs from globalist scholarship because globalist scholars tend to compare international

processes and structures assuming that their impact is homogeneous; such scholars also tend to *not* recognize how such processes and structures are variable, multidirectional, and interactional. Globalist scholars may use a worlds' system approach (i.e., First World, Second World, Third World, Fourth World); while such an approach is certainly useful for making connections between, for example, indigenous members residing in various parts of the Fourth World, recognizing a common struggle for land rights and political sovereignty, its model cannot make connections between middle-class U.S. workers and maquiladora workers in Tijuana, who in fact may also be indigenous. A transnational studies analysis sees these two groups of workers (although different based on class, geopolitical location, and potentially race) not as homogeneous but distinctly linked groups of people who are connected due to the transnational economy.

6. Neoliberal trade policies have had uneven impacts across nations and often have ended up bolstering the wealth of already wealthy nations. For example, NAFTA is a quintessential neoliberal transnational policy. Because the United States and Mexico, for example, are exempt from paying taxes and tariffs on goods traded between them, Mexico's social infrastructure has been grossly compromised, as the Mexican government is unable to provide social services to many of its citizens.

7. Although rhetorical scholars such as Jeff Rice (see "What Should College English Be?") and Colin Brooke (see *Lingua Fracta*) have begun to talk about how rhetorical scholars should consider how rhetorics are networked to and associated with less obvious texts, my theorizing of the network starts with transnational feminists' theorizing on gender and networked power relationships.

8. Although Eileen Schell and Wendy Hesford, for example, recently edited a special issue of *College English* that focused on transnational feminism and rhetorical studies, no book-length rhetorical studies have considered how contemporary globalization calls for new ways of analyzing gendered rhetorics and new rhetorical methodologies to examine how texts are written and received across geopolitical locales.

9. J. K. Gibson-Graham are actually two women (Katherine Gibson and Julie Graham) who choose to write under one name; thus I refer at times to them as one author and others as two authors.

10. Min-Zhan Lu and Bruce Horner have recently begun to consider globalization in their exploration of composition pedagogy. They make connections between our pedagogical practices during an evolving financial crisis, the rise of neoliberalism, and the permeation of borders.

11. My argument about the importance of feminist rhetoricians examining the circulation of rhetorics extends Mary Queen's analysis of the circulation of digital texts. In her essay "Transnational Feminist Rhetorics in a Digital World," Queen traces digital representations of the women's rights organization the Revolutionary Association of Women of Afghanistan (RAWA). She examines how women's self-representations become transformed and then fixed in a neoliberal framework of democracy and women's rights despite the multiple ways these women represented themselves in this organization. Queen ultimately seeks to bring feminist rhetorical study to the circulation of digital texts.

12. In the last decade, rhetoricians have begun to consider what rhetorical analysis might bring to public policy analysis. For example, in 2000, *Technical Communication Quarterly* dedicated an entire issue to the study of public policy writing; however, most authors focus on how technical communication scholars should write, teach, or intervene in public policy making. More recently, rhetorical scholars such as Elizabeth C. Britt,

Cynthia Selfe, Robert Asen, and J. Blake Scott have produced books examining specific U.S. policy practices—in Britt's case, a Massachusetts infertility law; in Selfe's, national technology and literacy education initiatives; in Asen's, how images of "the welfare queen" are visually and rhetorically constructed through the practices and texts of welfare policy; and in Scott's, mandated HIV/AIDS testing practices. Overall, these studies are important because they both demonstrate how the rhetoric of public policy is a normalizing force that frames individual's corporeal experiences and epistemologies, *and* they show the very material effects of the arguments that structure public policy. In particular, Britt's study considers how the rhetoric of legal definitions function to frame the way people describe, and even feel, about their experiences with infertility. She observes how policy making effects and is affected by audience members' prior conditioning. Likewise Scott examines the way health policy discourses work as a disciplinary force that categorize individuals as "normal" (healthy) and "deviant" (sick). The categories that Scott considers can also be seen in several contemporary policy initiatives at the local, national, and global levels.

13. Scott, for example, examines public policy responses to post–9/11 bioterrorism. He focuses on how these responses help rhetoricians rethink the traditional rhetorical concept of kairos, demonstrating the need for the field to connect rhetorical analysis both to public policy and to geopolitical economics. And more recently, Scott and I compiled an edited collection, *The Megarhetorics of Global Development*, that seeks to extend rhetorical studies to development studies. Chapters in the collection examine how the term *development* is often invoked as a commonplace, with taken-for-granted meanings about growth, progress, and beneficial effects. The collection examines public policies (among other things) and in doing so unpacks the megarhetorics of global development to show that they are not a single totalizing discourse but numerous interwoven strands of argument that impact life on multiple levels and across translocal contexts. The collection offers a rhetorical analysis that can help untangle and explain the rhetorical structures, frames, appeals, and assumptions at work in development discourses.

14. In fact, one of the challenges of studying public policy rhetorically is that it is often impossible to name an author of a policy. While we can trace who introduced a specific policy, by the time a policy is enrolled the number of writers of a policy may be impossible to trace. In some instances researchers can note policy markups and trace these changes to a group of people, but often the policy archive does not mention the specific ways a new version of policy was brought to the legislative floor.

15. For example, in the United States while neoliberal welfare policies pass social services into the hand of contracted agencies, we see the state reasserting its power as policy makers attempt to pass antigay marriage legislation, for example. With the European Union's uniting, we see state power somewhat reduced just as social services are also passed on to private organizations.

CHAPTER TWO. GENDER MAINSTREAMING

1. The ideology of gender mainstreaming was not born at the Fourth World Conference on Women, per se, rather according to the Jean Monnet Program at the NYU School of Law, gender mainstreaming was a concept that UN officials had been developing since the Third World Conference on Women in 1985. In fact prior to the Fourth World Con-

ference on Women, several European nations had adopted some sort of gender mainstreaming initiatives. Despite this move in Europe, the idea of gender mainstreaming did not circulate transnationally until the Beijing conference. In Europe, individual nations created their own mainstreaming initiatives, and it was not until Beijing that participants recognized gender mainstreaming as a common policy paradigm that needed to traverse *across* nations.

2. *Rational choice* refers to a dominant theory in microeconomics that assumes that individuals make decisions according to a calculation of the positive and negative effects of a choice in order to maximize personal advantage.

3. A recent example of how structural adjustment creates inflated prices took place in Zimbabwe where reporters noted that citizens needed to bring several backpacks of the Zimbabwean dollars to purchase necessities like bread. In 2008, several news outlets reported that it took 65,000 Zimbabwean dollars to purchase one bottle of Coca-Cola.

4. Also, see, for example, Johanna Brenner, "Transnational Feminism and the Struggle for Global Justice," in *New Politics* (Winter 2003). She points out that organizations such as the WID have been concerned with the relationship between gender and development for over thirty years. It is important to recognize the proliferation of such organizing when examining the changing rhetoric of gender within World Bank materials.

5. For a good and recent example of this sort of representation, see CARE's campaign for empowerment of women through microloans (and my discussion of empowerment in chapter 4). For more on these sorts of representations, see Spivak; Briggs; and Spurr.

6. It is important to note that soon after the enrollment of the Personal Responsibility Act several new welfare policies were introduced, including the Healthy Marriages and Children Act and the Responsible Fatherhood Act.

CHAPTER THREE. FITNESS

1. Also see note 4 in chapter 1 for a longer discussion on how transnational feminists read power.

2. This is not to say that some people with disabilities do not desire personal autonomy; rather, I mean to say that the body with a disability demonstrates how *all* people are reliant upon personal, social, and economic networks for survival.

3. I only identify people with disabilities as separate from their gender category because the instances I examine throughout this chapter maintain this false distinction.

4. The Bank's institutional structure and (inter)national presence, its stated goals and arguments, and its implicit values demonstrate its complacency with the inherent class structure produced by capitalism and Western imperialism, a structure that relies upon a low-income working class to produce affordable goods for the middle and upper classes of the globe. Likewise, the World Bank's institutional practices as envisioned on the pamphlet cover reflect Georges Balandier's definition of a colonial situation: "the domination imposed by a foreign minority, 'racially' and culturally different, over a materially weaker indigenous majority in the name of a racial (or ethnic) and cultural superiority" (qtd. in Spurr 5–6), which is in the interest of exploitation of bodies and other resources.

5. Although there is an obvious text present in this first page, I have chosen to analyze it as it reads as a whole image since the literal words work so clearly against the "primitive" drawing that they must be read together.

6. The World Bank can be characterized as what Garland-Thomson calls the "normate," "the constructed identity of those who, by way of the bodily configurations and cultural capital they assume, can step into a position of authority and wield the power it grants them" (qtd. in Davis, *Bending Over Backwards* 38). Although the Bank is not a person as Garland-Thomson's use of the term suggests, her characterization adequately represents the relationship that the Bank has with Third World nations and people. Headquartered in Washington, D.C., where seven thousand of their ten thousand employees work, the World Bank is the largest development organization in the world. The World Bank has 184 member countries, yet outside of the United States there are only a hundred other Bank offices throughout the world. All Bank presidents have been U.S. citizens. While the World Bank is a lending and credit institution, is does not function as a traditional bank. Instead, First World counties supply money to the World Bank (the United States is the largest contributor), and the Bank in turn provides loans to countries who agree to follow the Bank's development plans to become viable actors in the transnational economy. In this way, "normate" correctly characterizes the Bank because at the very least, the Bank, with its leadership and location in the United States, demonstrates its cultural and economic capital and how its body politic is well endowed with resources enabling its programs.

7. Students are often very savvy readers of images. In fact, my examination of the cultural narrative that the images in the *World Bank Group* pamphlet comes from a discussion I had in a second-level writing class. We were examining images in a recent issue of *National Geographic* when one student noted that images in the magazine did not in any way really reflect the textual narrative that accompanied the images. As a class we considered why this was the case. My students seemed to assume that images are much easier to read quickly than text. Thus, they concluded that *National Geographic*'s audience probably gleans most of their information from a quick "reading" of images. These students' important observation demonstrates the importance of reading images such as those produced by the Bank critically because they carry the important weight of communicating information and arguments in a quick and seemingly simple way.

8. Part of my description of the Bank's photos comes from Bhabha's description of colonial discourses whereby he lays out the discourse's paradoxical modes of representations and stereotypes (66). However, as I describe further and later in this chapter, colonial narratives function to persuade audiences due to their enthymematic mode of representation. Yet, due to the time frame and global economics of the later twentieth century, colonial discourse cannot be seen as merely static; rather it dynamically employs that which is familiar and unquestioned *and* that which appears to move certain people in the twenty-first century.

9. As I discuss at length in chapter 2, in this example we also see a rhetorical shift from liberal discourses—with an emphasis on aid and helping people with disabilities—to neoliberal discourses—with an emphasis on personal responsibility for accommodation (see Jung; Garland-Thomson; and Davis for more on this discourse). As I will explore further in chapter 4, we see another rendition of neoliberal charity discourses whereby people with resources are asked to give gifts to the poor in the name of personal responsibility or to be responsible to the poor and teaching the poor how to be responsible to themselves.

10. The Bank does realize that stigma is a major factor for integrating people with disabilities into their development plans too.

11. I want to point out that, indeed, we sometimes are unable to observe a disability; disabilities can be physical—sometimes visible, sometimes not—and mental. Thus, I say "see" here because the representation of this group of people with disabilities is significant.

CHAPTER FOUR. EMPOWERMENT

1. *Structural adjustment* is a term used to describe the policy changes for low-income nations put into effect by the World Bank or IMF to deal with a nation's fiscal imbalances. Structural adjustment programs (SAP) are part of the conditions for a nation to get new loans or to have prior loan's interest lowered. In general, SAPs tend to promote free market and neoliberal structural changes and thus countries often are made to privatize social and municipal programs, liberalize trade, and cut in-kind programs.

2. For example, the mission statement of the Fourth World Conference on Women states that its "Platform for Action is an agenda for women's empowerment" (*Beijing Declaration* 1). Likewise, as I noted in chapter 1, in 1997, the World Bank made "women's empowerment" a key initiative in their gender mainstreaming development programs. Additionally, the Third Millennial Development Goal adopted by the UN, the World Bank, and other supranational and NGOs seeks to "promote gender equality and women's empowerment" (see the Millennium Development Goals). In 2001, for example, India enrolled the National Policy for the Empowerment of Women, a policy document intended to strengthen their already gender-attendant national constitution. As I explored briefly in chapter 2, within the United States, national welfare policies employed a rhetoric of empowerment in their push to move poor women from unpaid domestic labor to paid labor outside the home. And, more recently, Sherifa Zuhur and the Army War College Strategic Studies Institute published the report *Iraq, Women's Empowerment, and Public Policy*, which addresses Iraqi and Kurdish women's needs during Iraq's governmental reconstruction.

3. See, for example, Schell; Hesford, "Global Turns" and "Kairos"; and Hesford and Schell, "Configurations of Transnationality."

4. The idea that access to money levels the playing field for men and women is an idea that is also seen as part of the justification for giving women microloans.

5. It is important to note that if a particular group of women wanted to focus on the relationship between gender equality and economics then a GAD approach would support that and might even work to help that group apply for a World Bank loan to support their efforts. The notion that "gender equality is smart economics" is not outside of an empowerment paradigm per se, unless it is imposed from above without the consent or wishes of the women themselves.

6. Also see chapter 2 of this book for more on how the World Bank definition of mainstreaming includes drawing from women's social capital.

7. Microcredit loans are paid back with interest, but most microfinance companies and organizations do not oversee what the women do with the loans although often these same organizations may offer education programs ranging from debit repayment to local health issues.

8. The self-help groups were part of a three-tiered plan that also included creating a community investment fund to help expand public goods (such as water and roads) and extend the support of private sector to help social sector anti-poverty programs.

9. In addition, Isserles reports that women who receive microloans do not tend to fare well after they receive the loans. Many women reported an increase in domestic violence when women refused to give their loan money to their husbands and because they challenged the gender hierarchies in the family. Women also reported that loan officers tended to coerce women into repayment, making these same women seek loans from other agencies and thereby creating a cycle of borrowing and debt (Isserles 49).

10. While Kiva makes it seem as though dollars go through their organization directly into the hands of individual people with business plans, Kiva actually partners with local microfinance agencies that provide the money to entrepreneurs and then collect interest from them. Kiva does provide a networking platform (on their website) so that people who have provided money to borrowers can get reports from the borrower about how the money is being used or how a project thrived or not. Borrowers are encouraged to write messages to their lenders through this platform.

WORKS CITED

2004 World Survey on the Role of Women in Development: Women and International Migration. New York: United Nations Department of Economic and Social Affairs, 2006. Web. 1 July 2010.

Albright, Madeleine Korbel, Hillary Rodham Clinton, and President's Interagency Council on Women (U.S.). *America's Commitment: Women 2000.* DIANE Publishing, 2000.

Alexander, M. Jacqui. *Pedagogies of Crossing: Meditations on Feminism, Sexual Politics, Memory, and the Sacred.* Durham: Duke University Press, 2005.

Archibald, George. "World's Women Convene." *Washington Times,* 5 Sept. 1995: A1.

Asen, Robert. *Visions of Poverty: Welfare Policy and Political Imagination.* East Lansing: Michigan State University Press, 2002.

Ault, Amber, and Eve Sandberg. "Our Policies, Their Consequence: Zambian Women's Lives under Structural Adjustment." *An Introduction to Women's Studies: Gender in a Transnational World.* Ed. Inderpal Grewal and Caren Kaplan. New York: McGraw-Hill, 2006. 69–71.

Bacchi, Carol, and Joan Eveline. "Mainstreaming and Neoliberalism: A Contested Relationship." *Mainstreaming Politics: Gendering Practices and Feminist Theory.* Ed. Carol Bacchi and Joan Eveline. Adelaide: University of Adelaide Press, 2010.

Bahri, Deepika. "Terms of Engagement: Postcolonialism, Transnationalism, and Composition Studies." *Crossing Borderlands: Composition and Postcolonial Studies.* Ed. Andrea Lunsford and Lahoucine Ouzgane. Pittsburgh: University of Pittsburgh Press, 2004. 67–83.

Bedford, Kate. "Loving to Straighten out Development: Sexuality and Ethnodevelopment in the World Bank's Ecuadorian Lending." *Feminist Legal Studies* 13.3 (2005): 295–322. Web.

Beijing Declaration and Platform for Action. Fourth World Conference on Women, Beijing 1995. United Nations, 2005. Web. http://www.un.org/womenwatch/daw/beijing/pdf/BDPfA%20E.pdf.

Bergeron, Suzanne. "Challenging the World Bank's Narrative of Inclusion." *World Bank Literature.* Ed. Amativa Kumar. Minneapolis: University of Minnesota Press, 2003.

———. *Fragments of Development: Nation, Gender, and the Space of Modernity.* Ann Arbor: University of Michigan Press, 2004.

Bhabha, Homi K. *The Location of Culture.* London: Routledge, 1994.

Bitzer, Lloyd F. "The Rhetorical Situation." *Philosophy and Rhetoric* 1.1 (1968): 1–14.

———. "The Rhetorical Situation." *Philosophy and Rhetoric,* supplement 25 (1992): 1–14.

Briggs, Laura. *Reproducing Empire: Race, Sex, Science, and U.S. Imperialism in Puerto Rico.* Berkeley: University of California Press, 2002.

Britt, Elizabeth Carol. *Conceiving Normalcy: Rhetoric, Law, and the Double Binds of Infertility.* Tuscaloosa: University of Alabama Press, 2001.

Brooke, Collin Gifford. *Lingua Fracta: Toward a Rhetoric of New Media.* Cresskill: Hampton, 2009.

Brown, Wendy. "Neo-liberalism and the End of Liberal Democracy." *Theory & Event* 7.1 (2003). *Project MUSE*. Web. 15 Feb. 2011.

———. *Regulating Aversion: Tolerance in the Age of Identity and Empire*. Princeton: Princeton University Press, 2006.

Cairo Programme of Action. "Summary of the Programme of Action of the International Conference on Population and Development: 5–13 September 1994." *Earth Negotiations Bulletin* 6.39 (1994). Web.

Carelton, Sue Ellen. "Development as History and Process." *Women, Gender, and Development Reader*. Ed. Nalini Visvanathan, Lynn Duggan, Laurie Nisonoff, and Nan Wiegersma. Atlantic Highlands: Zed Books, 1997.

Clinton, Hillary Rodham. "Remarks for the United Nations Fourth World Conference on Women." 5 Sept. 1995. Web.

Collins, Patricia H. *Black Feminist Thought: Knowledge, Consciousness, and the Politics of Empowerment*. London: Routledge, 1991.

Cooppan, Vilashini. "The Ruins of Empire: The National and Global Politics of America's Return to Rome." *Postcolonial Studies and Beyond*. Ed. Ania Loomba, Suvir Kaul, Matti Bunzl, et al. Durham: Duke University Press, 2005. 80–100.

Davis, Lennard J. *Bending Over Backwards: Disability, Dismodernism, and Other Difficult Positions*. New York: New York University Press, 2002.

———. *Enforcing Normalcy: Disability, Deafness, and the Body*. London: Verso, 1995.

Deprez, Luisa Stormer. *The Family Support Act of 1988: A Case Study of Welfare Policy in the 1980s*. Lewiston: Edwin Mellen, 2002.

Dev, S. Mahendra, and P. Padmanabha Rao. *Poverty Alleviation Programmes in Andhra Pradesh—An Assessment*. Begumpet, Hyderabad: Centre for Economic and Social Studies, N. O. Campus, 2002.

Dingo, Rebecca, and J. Blake Scott, ed. *Megarhetorics of Global Development*. Pittsburgh: University of Pittsburgh Press, 2012.

Duggan, Lisa. *The Twilight of Equality: Neoliberalism, Cultural Politics, and the Attack on Democracy*. Boston: Beacon Press, 2003.

Ecuador Gender Review: Issues and Recommendations. Washington, D.C: World Bank, 2000.

Edbauer, Jenny. "Unframing Models of Public Distribution: From Rhetorical Situation to Rhetorical Ecologies." *RSQ: Rhetoric Society Quarterly* 35.4 (2005): 5–24. Web.

Ede, Lisa, and Andrea Lunsford. "Audience Addressed/Audience Invoked: The Role of Audience in Composition Theory and Pedagogy." *College Composition and Communication* 35.2 (1984): 155–71.

Fernando, Jude L. "Nongovernmental Organizations, Micro-Credit, and Empowerment of Women." *Annals of the American Academy of Political and Social Science* 554.1 (1997): 150–77.

Fukuyama, Francis. *The End of History and the Last Man*. New York: Free, 1992.

From Exclusion to Inclusion. World Bank, 2004. DVD.

Garland-Thomson, Rosemarie. *Extraordinary Bodies: Figuring Physical Disability in American Culture and Literature*. New York: Columbia University Press, 1997.

———. "The Politics of Staring: Visual Rhetorics of Disability in Popular Photography." *Disability Studies: Enabling the Humanities*. Ed. Sharon L Snyder, Brenda Jo Brueggemann, and Rosemarie Garland-Thomson. New York: Modern Language Association of America, 2002.

George, Susan. "A Short History of Neoliberalism: Twenty Years of Elite Economics and Emerging Opportunities for Structural Change." *Global Finance: New Thinking on Regulating Speculative Capital Markets*. Ed. Walden F Bello, Nicola Bullard, and Kamal Malhotra. Dhaka, Bangladesh: St. Martins, 2000.

Gibson-Graham, J. K. *A Postcapitalist Politics*. Minneapolis: University of Minnesota Press, 2006.

Giddens, Anthony. *The Third Way: The Renewal of Social Democracy*. Cambridge: Polity, 1998.

Gjelten, Tom. "Global Reality Challenges IMF's Free Market Gospel." *NPR*. 18 March 2010. Web. http://www.npr.org/templates/story/story.php?storyId=124792660.

Grameen Bank. "Village Phones." *Annual Report 2007*. 21 June 2009. Grameen Communications. Web.

Gramsci, Antonio. "The Modern Prince: Analysis of Situations, Relations of Force." *Selections from the Prison Notebooks*. New York: International Publishers, 1971.

Grewal, Inderpal. *Transnational America: Feminisms, Diasporas, Neoliberalisms*. Durham: Duke University Press, 2005.

Hahn, Harlan. "Advertising the Acceptably Employable Image." *The Disability Studies Reader*. Ed. Lennard J Davis. New York: Routledge, 1997. 172–86.

Halfron, Saul. *The Cairo Consensus: Demographic Surveys, Women's Empowerment, and Regime Change in Population Policy*. Lanham: Lexington Books, 2006.

Hardt, Michael, and Antonio Negri. *Empire*. Cabridge: Harvard University Press, 2001.

Hesford, Wendy S. "Global Turns and Cautions in Rhetoric and Composition Studies." *PMLA* 121.3 (2006): 787–801.

———. "Kairos and the Geopolitical Rhetorics of Global Sex Work and Video Advocacy." *Just Advocacy? Women's Human Rights, Transnational Feminism, and the Politics of Representation*. Ed. Wendy S. Hesford and Wendy Kozol. Piscataway: Rutgers University Press, 2005. 146–94.

Hesford, Wendy S., and Eileen E. Schell. "Configurations of Transnationality: Locating Feminist Rhetorics." *College English* 70.5 (2008): 461–70.

Hesford, Wendy S., and Wendy Kozol. "Introduction." *Just Advocacy? Women's Human Rights, Transnational Feminism, and the Politics of Representation*. Ed. Wendy S. Hesford and Wendy Kozol. Piscataway: Rutgers University Press, 2005. 146–94.

Integrating Women into National Economies ("Percy Amendment"). Section 113. Foreign Assistance Act of 1961. Pub. L. 87–195. 4 September 1961. Stat. 75.424.

Isserles, Robin G. "Microcredit: The Rhetoric of Empowerment, the Reality of 'Development as Usual.'" *Women's Studies Quarterly* 31.3 (2003): 38–57.

Jaggar, Alison M. "Is Globalization Good for Women?" *Comparative Literature* 53.4 (2001): 298–314.

Jung, Julie. "Textual Mainstreaming and Rhetorics of Accommodation." *Rhetoric Review* 26.2 (2007): 160.

Kaplan, Caren. *Questions of Travel: Postmodern Discourses of Displacement*. Durham: Duke University Press, 1996.

Kaplan, Caren, and Inderpal Grewal, ed. *Scattered Hegemonies: Postmodernity and Transnational Feminist Practices*. Minneapolis: University of Minneapolis Press, 1994.

Kerr, Joanna. "From 'WID' to 'GAD' to Women's Rights: The First Twenty Years of AWID." *AWID's Occasional Paper Series* 9 (2002). Web.

Kiva. 2005–2009. "What is Kiva?" kiva.org/about. Web.

Kristof, Nicholas D., and Sheryl WuDunn. *Half the Sky: Turning Women's Oppression into Opportunity for Women World Wide.* New York: Vintage Press, 2010.

Kvam, Reider. *Gender-Responsive Social Analysis: A Guidance Note.* Washington, D.C.: Social Development Department, World Bank, 2005. Web.

Latour, Bruno. *Reassembling the Social: An Introduction to Actor-Network-Theory.* New York: Oxford University Press, 2005.

Levitt, Peggy, and Sanjeev Khagram, ed. *The Transnational Studies Reader: Interdisciplinary Intersections and Innovations.* London: Routledge, 2008.

Lu, Min-Zhin, and Bruce Horner. "Composing in a Global-Local Context: Careers, Mobility, Skills." *College English* 72.2 (2009): 113–33.

Lutz, Catherine, and Jane Lou Collins. *Reading National Geographic.* Chicago: University of Chicago Press, 1993.

Mayoux, Linda. "Questioning Virtuous Spirals: Micro-Finance and Women's Empowerment in Africa." *Journal of International Development* 11.7 (1999): 957–84.

McIntosh, C. Alison, and Jason L. Finkle. "The Cairo Conference on Population and Development: A New Paradigm?" *Population and Development Review* 21.2 (1995): 223–60.

McRuer, Robert. "Taking It to the Bank: Independence and Inclusion on the World Market." *Journal of Literary & Cultural Disability Studies* 1.2 (2007): 5–14.

Millennium Development Goals. Department of Public Information, United Nations, 2008. Web. http://www.un.org/millenniumgoals.

Moghadam, Valentine M. *Globalizing Women: Transnational Feminist Networks.* Baltimore: Johns Hopkins University Press, 2005.

Mohanty, Chandra Talpade. *Feminism without Borders: Decolonizing Theory, Practicing Solidarity.* Durham: Duke University Press, 2003.

Momsen, Janet Henshall. *Gender and Development.* New York: Routledge, 2010.

Naples, Nancy A., and Manisha Desai, ed. *Women's Activism and Globalization: Linking Struggles and Transnational Politics.* New York: Routledge, 2002.

Narayan, Uma. *Dis-Locating Cultures: Identities, Traditions, and Third-World Feminism.* New York: Routledge, 1997.

Nelson, Barbara J. *Making an Issue of Child Abuse: Political Agenda Setting for Social Problems.* Chicago: University of Chicago Press, 1984.

The Nobel Foundation. *The Nobel Peace Prize 2006.* 2009. Nobel Web AB. Web. http://nobelprize.org/nobel_prizes/peace/laureates/2006.

Our Bodies, Ourselves. 2005–2009. Boston's Women's Health Collective, Inc. Web. http://www.ourbodiesourselves.org.

Personal Responsibility and Work Opportunity Reconciliation Act of 1996. 104th Congress. 2nd Session. H.R. 3734. 21 August 1996.

Pineda, V., and M. Fried. *A World Enabled: Disability as a Human Rights Issue.* San Francisco: Babylon Arts Group and Public Interest TV Films, 2004. DVD.

Queen, Mary. "Transnational Feminist Rhetorics in a Digital World." *College English* 70.5 (2008): 471–89.

Rice, Jeff. "Networks and New Media." *College English* 69.2 (2006): 127–33.

Riedner, Rachel, and Kevin Mahoney. *Democracies to Come: Rhetorical Action, Neoliberalism, and Communities of Resistance.* Lanham: Lexington Books, 2008.

Rittich, Kerry. *Recharacterizing Restructuring: Law, Distribution, and Gender in Market Reform.* Erik Castren Institute Monographs on International Law and Human Rights. Ed. Martti Koskenniemi. Vol. 3. The Hague: Kluwer Law International, 2002.

Rose, Nikolas, and Peter Miller. *Governing the Present: Administering Economic, Social and Personal Life.* Cambridge: Polity, 2008.

Rowlands, Jo. "A Word of the Times, but What Does It Mean? Empowerment in the Discourse and Practice of Development." *Women and Empowerment: Illustrations from the Third World.* Ed. Haleh Afshar. New York: St. Martins, 1998. 11–34.

Schell, Eileen E. "Gender, Rhetorics, and Globalization: Rethinking the Spaces and Locations of Women's Rhetorics in Our Field." *Teaching Rhetorica: Theory, Pedagogy, Practice.* Ed. Kate Ronald and Joy S. Ritchie. Portsmouth: Boynton/Cook Heinemann, 2006. 160–74.

Scott, J. Blake. *Risky Rhetoric: AIDS and the Cultural Practices of HIV Testing.* Carbondale: Southern Illinois University Press, 2003.

Selfe, Cynthia L. *Technology and Literacy in the Twenty-First Century: The Importance of Paying Attention.* Carbondale: Southern Illinois University Press, 1999.

Spivak, Gayatri Chakravorty. "Can the Subaltern Speak?" *Marxism and the Interpretation of Culture.* Ed. Cary Nelson and Lawrence Grossberg. Urbana: University of Illinois Press, 1988.

———. *A Critique of Postcolonial Reason: Toward a History of the Vanishing Present.* Cambridge: Harvard University Press, 1999.

Spurr, David. *The Rhetoric of Empire: Colonial Discourse in Journalism, Travel Writing, and Imperial Administration.* Durham: Duke University Press, 1993.

Stone-Mediatore, Shari. *Reading across Borders: Storytelling and Knowledges of Resistance.* New York: Palgrave Macmillan, 2003.

Steger, Manfred B., and Ravi K. Roy. *Neoliberalism: A Very Short Introduction.* New York: Oxford University Press, 2010.

Tefft, Sheila. "War Over Words Divides UN Women's Conference." *Christian Science Monitor* 87.200 (1995): 6.

Terry, Jennifer. *An American Obsession: Science, Medicine, and Homosexuality in Modern Society.* Chicago: University of Chicago Press, 1999.

"Transcoding." *Wikipedia.* 14 June 2010. Web.

Trimbur, John. "Composition and the Circulation of Writing." *College Composition and Communication* 52.2 (2000): 188–219.

True, Jacqui, and Michael Mintrom. "Transnational Networks and Policy Diffusion: The Case of Gender Mainstreaming." *International Studies Quarterly* 45.1 (2001): 27–57. Web.

Tsing, Anna Lowenhaupt. *Friction: An Ethnography of Global Connection.* Princeton: Princeton University Press, 2005.

Ukeles, Jacob B. "Policy Analysis: Myth or Reality?" *Public Administration Review* 37.3 (1977): 223–28.

Waldman, Peter. "Lost in Translation: How to 'Empower Women' in Chinese." *Wall Street Journal,* 13 Sept. 1994: A1.

Welch, Nancy. "Living Room: Teaching Public Writing in a Post-Publicity Era." *College Composition and Communication* 56.3 (2005): 470–92.

Wilson, James C., and Cynthia Lewiecki-Wilson. *Embodied Rhetorics: Disability in Language and Culture.* Carbondale: Southern Illinois University Press, 2001.

Wolfensohn, James D. "The Challenge of Inclusion." 1997. Web.

———. "Disability and Development: Opening Remarks." 2004. Web.

World Bank. *Advancing Gender Equality: World Bank Action since Beijing.* Washington, D.C.: World Bank, 2000. Web.

———. "Andhra Pradesh District Poverty Initiatives Project (Velugu)." *Worldbank.org.* 12 August 2002. Web.

———. "Disability—Frequently Asked Questions." *Worldbank.org.* 19 Nov. 2009. Web.

———. *Engendering Development through Gender Equality in Rights, Resources, and Voice.* Washington, D.C.: Oxford University Press, 2001.

———. *Implementation Completion Report (TF-25388 TF-26592 IDA-32480) on a Credit in the Amount of US$90 Million to the Islamic Republic of Pakistan for a Poverty Alleviation Fund Project.* Report Number 32513. Finance and Private Sector Development Unit, South Asia Region, 15 June 2005.

———. *Project Appraisal Document on a Proposed Credit in the Amount of SDR 82.9 Million (US$111.0 Million Equivalent) to India for the Andhra Pradesh District Poverty Initiatives Project.* Report Number 20089-IN. SASRD, South Asia Regional Office, 20 Mar. 2000.

———. *Toward Gender Equality: The Role of Public Policy.* Washington, D.C: World Bank, 1995.

———. *World Bank Group: Working for a World Free of Poverty.* Washington, D.C: World Bank, 2003.

Wroughton, Lesley. "Third World Concepts No Longer Relevant." *Reuters.* 14 April 2010. Web.

Zuhur, Sherifa, and Army War College (U.S.) Strategic Studies Institute. *Iraq, Women's Empowerment, and Public Policy.* Carlisle: Strategic Studies Institute, U.S. Army War College, 2006. Web.

INDEX